GLOBAL BUSINESS ENGLISH

by Prof. Yang-kee LEE

for
International Trade and
Business Correspondence

도서출판 청람

Preface

During the last ten-years, the gale for English classes(lectures) has been raging in universities. It is true that it doesn't really make sense for people whose mother tongue is not English, to lecture in English and students take their class. However, from the point of view of globalization and internationalization, it is not easy to deny that English has become the official language of the world and business.

I have had an interest in English since childhood but I haven't had experience studying in British-American countries. I was in China between 2005~2007 as a visiting professor and learned Chinese at a college language school for 4 semesters. While I studied Chinese, I felt keenly the necessity of knowing foreign languages; in particular I developed a more rounded belief regarding the importance of English.

After returning to Korea, despite a lack of previous experience lecturing in English, I started teaching English classes at three universities in Busan. With a steady effort, solid accomplishments were made. At that time, it was rare to have a textbook in English, hence I regularly stayed awake creating suitable material, and I feel the effort was worth it for my students. To this end, I really appreciate and thank all the students who studied and made efforts to learn English over the many years I have been a teaching professor.

Through preparing English lectures, I have considered how to kill 2 birds with one stone. The first being Knowledge Transmission of the Major and the second being Improvement in a Foreign Language, namely English.

First, I tried to harmonize specialized knowledge for International Commerce and

Business English. Through harmonizing theory and practice, I was able to mould them together in a meaningful and understandable way.

Second, I used Standard English to write accurate and meaningful English documents to help students engage in common international standards.

Third, I continued to work hard so I was be able to present, make/receive phone calls and engage in face to face conversations in English.

Fourth, the fact that all the contents of textbooks are written in English puts a great burden on students who are not familiar with English or teachers who have to explain the contents to students. So, the main contents were added with minimal Korean explanations.

Even if there are deficiencies, I will consistently try to improve my lecturing in English and English textbooks based on feed forward from others. I hope through this book, that students will also be able to kill 2 birds with one stone.

Yang-Kee Lee
Busan, KOREA
August 2023

Contents

Chapter 09 | Implementation Phase: Marine Insurance

Chapter 10 | Implementation Phase: International Payment

Chapter 11 | Follow-up Phase

Chapter 12 | English Resume

1

CHAPTER

Global Business English

Fundamentals of Global Business

1-1 Concept of Global Business

1-2 Types of Global Business

1-3 The Procedures for Global Business

Chapter 1

Fundamentals of Global Business

Key Sentences

Global business refers to international trade. International trade is the exchange of goods and services among individuals and businesses in multiple countries.

Objectives

After studying this lesson, you will be able to:

- understand the definition of global business
- identify various types of global business
- explain the procedures for global business

1-1 Concept of Global Business

글로벌 비즈니스는 국제무역을 의미한다. 국제무역은 여러 국가에 있는 개인과 기업 간에 상품과 서비스를 교환하는 것을 말한다. 또한 여러 국가 간에 비즈니스를 수행하는 최종 기업 또는 국제 비즈니스 회사와 같은 특정 주체를 의미한다. 상품이나 서비스의 흐름에 대한 일반적인 관행과 채널에 관련된 다국적 당사자 간에는 다양한 유형의 글로벌 비즈니스 또는 국제무역이 있다.

Global business refers to international trade. International trade is the exchange of goods and services among individuals and businesses in multiple countries. It also means a specific entity, such as a multinational corporation or international business company that engages in business among multiple countries. The exchange of goods over great distances goes back a very long time. Anthropologists have already established long-distance trading in Europe in the Stone Age. Sea-borne trading was commonplace in many regions of the world in times predating Greek civilization. Such trade, of course, was not by definition "global" but had the same characteristics. In the 16th century all of the continents came to be routinely linked by ocean-based communications. Trading activity in the modern sense rapidly followed at the beginning of the 17th century; it might be more accurate to say that it "returned" again because trading of such character had taken place in Roman times as well.

Business refers to any human activity undertaken on a regular basis with the object to earn profit or monetary gain through production, distribution, sale or purchase of goods and services. Business may also be defined as "an activity involving regular production or purchase of goods and services for sale, transfer and exchange with an object of earning profit."

1-2 Types of Global Business

글로벌 비즈니스의 유형에는 수출입, 라이선스, 프랜차이즈, 관리계약, 턴키운영, 해외직접투자 등이 있다.

There are many different types of global business or international trade between multi-national parties involved in the common practices and the channels for the flow of goods or services. They include the specific types of import and export transactions or other transaction methods depending upon the categorisation of items and the degree of involved parties. For instance, visible trade refers to the exchange of physically tangible goods between countries, involving the export, import, and re-export of goods at various stages of production. It is distinguished from invisible trade, which involves the export and import of physically intangible items such as services.

Another example is direct trade or bilateral trade which refers to a system of trading between two parties from different countries attempting to balance its trade with that of the other. It is different from indirect trade, which requires the involvement of a third party, and it includes intermediate trade, merchandising trade, transit trade (passing trade), and switch trade, etc. There is also counter trade and it means exchanging goods or services which are paid for, in whole or part, with other goods or services, rather than with money. This includes barter trade, compensation trade, triangular trade, and counter purchase.

In general, a firm can sell a physical product abroad in terms of export or can locate a production facility abroad via foreign direct investment(FDI). There is an array of intermediate types of global business that can allow a firm to acquire global or international returns on its unique advantages. These are as follows.

(1) Exporting/Importing

It is a type of global business selling a physical product and receiving sales price in return, unless it is done in the way of counter trade. It only entails foreign marketing and documentation from domestic operations without significant changes. Little investment, typically no investment abroad, is required. However, it is susceptible to trade barriers and exchange rate fluctuation. It also has logistical difficulties and is less suitable for service products. Import is the act of bringing goods into a country. Importing is defined as goods and services produced by host country and purchased by parent country. it is reverse process of Exports.

(2) Licensing

It deals with technical information, assistance, and/or using rights. In return, it collects a licensing fee and allows it to use the information or rights. It is advantageous for increasing a return on investment in technology, creativity, or customer relations. It also requires little additional capital or time investment. However, the downside is that the agreement generally prohibits the originating firm from exploiting the assets in particular foreign markets. It is also difficult to manage quality control.

(3) Franchising

This type of business transacts its trademark, on-going service, some inputs and shared marketing expenses. In return, it is given payment for the trademark, payment for inputs used, and a share of operating revenue or profits. There are three main advantages. Firstly, it is an important way of gaining foreign returns on certain kinds of customer services and trade name assets. Secondly, it allows some control over the conditions of sale in the foreign market. Finally, it only entails a limited financial commitment. However, quality control is weak.

(4) Management Contracts

It involves interacting with people for a certain period of time. In return for this, it receives a salary, benefits and indirect costs, as well as a share of operating revenues or profits. This type has both pros and cons. The contractor puts up no capital and bears no risk. It is also useful in foreign contexts which prohibit FDI or FDI is too risky. However, the contractee has a good chance to become a competitor, at least in the local market.

(5) Turn-key Operation

It offers design, construction and equipping of a production facility to the trading partner. In return, it takes all costs plus fees, assumption of ownership and risk at the end of the project. As the contractor bears no risk in this type of business, it is useful in foreign contexts prohibit FDI or FDI is too risky. However, the contractee might have a good chance to become a competitor, at least in the local market.

(6) Foreign Direct Investment(FDI)

This type of business provides capital, management, technology, and perhaps key material inputs. As a reward, it collects repatriated profits, licensing fees and transfer payments for inputs. It is profitable, relatively easy to handle quality control and has the possibility of tax avoidance through transfer pricing. However, it is not easy to acquire capital or an operating commitment.

1-3 The Procedures for Global Business

수출절차(신용장방식)

① 수출물품을 선정한다.
② 수출시장을 조사한다.
③ 수출승인이나 수출요건을 확인한다.
④ 바이어를 선정하고 수출계약을 체결한다.
⑤ 수출신용장을 접수한다.
⑥ 수출물품을 조달하고 무역금융을 이용한다.
⑦ 수출검사와 포장을 실시한다.
⑧ 해상운송 및 해상보험계약을 체결한다.
⑨ 수출통관절차를 시작한다.
⑩ 물품을 선적한다.
⑪ 수출대금을 회수한다.
⑫ 관세환급을 신청한다.

수입절차(신용장방식)
① 수입물품을 선정한다.
② 수입승인과 수입요건을 확인한다.
③ 해외거래처를 물색한다.
④ 수입계약을 체결한다.
⑤ 수입신용장을 발행한다.
⑥ 대금결제 및 선적서류를 인수한다.
⑦ 수입통관 및 물품을 수령한다.

This General Procedures for Export and Import is based on L/C(Letter of Credit).

1. Overseas Market Research

① Exporter "A" looks for business connections abroad through his Commercial Travellers, Chamber of Commerce, Exchange Banks, Business Friends, Business Directories, Internet, etc.

② Exporter "A" dispatches to the prospective importers his "Trade Circulars," enclosing catalogues and any other necessary information such as business reference.

③ Importer "B" inquires of the credit standing of the exporter "A" and exporter "A's" mode of doing business through exporter "A's" bank references or business references.

④ From which importer "B" may receive a satisfactory report on the credit and business standing of the firm.

⑤ Importer "B" inquires of several trade terms.

2. Formation and Conclusion of Contract

① Exporter "A" sends a firm offer to the Importer "B" by E-mail.

② Importer "B" makes a counter offer against the firm offer from the Exporter "A."

③ Exporter "A" makes a new firm offer against the counter offer from the

Importer “B.”

④ Importer “B” accepts the offer by E-mail and sends the order to the Exporter “A.”

⑤ Exporter “A” and importer B conclude a sales contract providing for payment by a Documentary Credit.

3. Implementation of Contract

① Importer “B” instructs the issuing bank to issue of a “documentary Letter of Credit(L/C)” in favor of the Exporter in order to facilitate drawing drafts.

② The Issuing Bank issues the documentary Letter of Credit and ask the advising bank to advice or confirm the documentary Letter of Credit.

③ Importer “B” notifies the Exporter “A” of the L/C issued.

④ The advising bank notifies the issuance of the L/C to the Exporter “A.”

⑤ When the Exporter receives a proper L/C, he will prepare for contracted goods. In other words, Exporter “A” buys the ordered goods from the local suppliers usually by Local L/C or credit account. Or Exporter “A” imports raw material from the overseas market in order to make the export goods.

⑥ Exporter “A” packs and marks the purchased goods for exportation, and makes “Invoices,” “Packing Lists”, “Shipping Request,” “Export Declaration.”

⑦ Exporter “A” obtains “Certificate of Weight and Measurement” from a Measurer’s Company, regarding the weight and measurement of the shipping cargo. Exporter “A” obtains “Inspection Certificate” from the Inspecting Authorities concerned.

⑧ Exporter “A” has to get “Consular Invoices” verified, if required he procures “Certificate of Origin,” “Inspection Certificate,” “Certificate of Health,” and other Certificates, if required.

⑨ Exporter “A” applies for the cargo space to a steamship company. Against Shipping Request(S/R), a “Shipping Order(S/O)” is issued.

⑩ Exporter “A” tenders to the Customs Authorities a set of “Export Declaration (E/D).” After the approval of the Export Declaration, an “Export Permit” is granted.

⑪ Exporter "A" loads the goods on board the vessel against the tender of the "Shipping Order" and the "Export Permit."

⑫ After the completion of the loading of the cargo, a "Mate's Receipt(M/R)" or "Dock Receipt(D/R) is issued and Export Permit is returned after having been stamped by the Customs officer on the spot to the effect that the loading had duly been completed.

⑬ "Bills of Lading(B/L)" are issued from the steamship company against the tender of M/R or D/R.

⑭ Exporter "A" applies marine insurance contract, tendering "Insurance Application" to the insurance company. Against the application, "Insurance Policy" or "Insurance Certificate" is issued.

⑮ Exporter "A" sends the required documents to the bank where the L/C is made available(nominating bank).

⑯ The nominating bank examines and compares related documents with the terms of L/C. If they meet the requirements of the L/C, the bank will pay, accept, or negotiated under the L/C.

⑰ The nominating bank sends the documents to the issuing bank.

⑱ Exporter "A" draws on "Drawee"(i.e. the L/C Issuing Bank) "Documentary Drafts" accompanied by full set of Bill of Lading, the Insurance Policy, the Commercial Invoices and other necessary documents in exact conformity with the terms of L/C.

⑲ Against the presentation of the Documentary Drafts to the Negotiating Bank, Exporter "A" receives the proceeds, the net value of the bill of exchange from the Negotiating Bank.

⑳ The Negotiating Bank dispatches the Documentary Drafts enclosing full set of Documents to L/C Issuing Bank.

㉑ Exporter "A" dispatches to the Importer "B" the "Advice of Shipment," enclosing one complete sets of nonnegotiable shipping documents.

㉒ The L/C Issuing Bank presents the draft to the Importer "B"

㉓ Upon the presentation of the draft, Importer "B" pays the bill if it is drawn under at sight or he accepts the bill if drawn under Usance.

㉔ Against the payment or acceptance of the bill, Importer "B" obtains the shipping documents from the bank.

㉕ Importer "B" tenders the B/L endorsed to the steamship company.

㉖ Against the tender of the B/L, Importer "B" obtains "Delivery Order(D/O)" from the shipping company.

㉗ Importer "B" tenders a set of "Import Declaration(I/D)" together with Commercial Invoices, "Certificate of Origin" if required, to the Customs Authorities.

㉘ An "Import Permit(I/P)" is granted when the import duties would have been paid if the goods dutiable.

㉙ Importer "B" tenders a "Declaration for Clearance" accompanied by the Import Permit together with D/O usually through the hand of a landing agent or a freight forwarder.

㉚ A "Clearance Permit" having been granted, Importer "B" takes delivery of the goods from the customs compound or directly from the steamship.

㉛ Importer "B" disposes of the imported goods to local clients.

㉜ Importer "B" pays the bill, if drawn under Usance, to the L/C Issuing Bank on its maturity day.

㉝ The L/C Issuing Bank remits the proceeds to the Negotiating Bank in the exporting country, thus the account is fully settled and the whole procedure is completed.

4. Claims and Dispute Settlement

Importer "B" lodges claims against damages or losses, if any, with the insurance company accompanied by a "Survey Report," "Insurance Policy" and other documents required. The claims will be indemnified against these documents.

Key Expressions & Technical Terms

✔ **Business Transaction**: A business transaction is an event that involves a financial transaction between different parties. Typically, this is a reciprocation against goods or services. Such transactions can either be a simple cash purchase or in the form of a contract.

✔ **Business Contract**: A Business contract is a legally binding agreement that lays out terms for the sale of goods or services between two companies. Business Contracts typically list what products or services are being sold and the price for each, as well as additional terms such as conditions, warranties, timelines, and payments.

* Commerce is the activity of buying and selling of goods and services, especially on a large scale. The system includes legal, economic, political, social, cultural and technological systems that are in operation in any country or internationally. Thus, commerce is a system or an environment that affects the business prospects of economies. It can also be defined as a component of business which includes all activities, functions and institutions involved in transferring goods from producers to consumers.

✔ **Commodity**: In economics, a commodity is a marketable item produced to satisfy wants or needs. Often the item is fungible. Economic commodities comprise goods and services.

✔ **International Business Law**: Cultivating transnational legal knowledge to promote efficient and effective professional services and guide businesses in a global community.

* Trade involves the transfer of the ownership of goods or services from one person or entity to another in exchange for other goods or services or for money.

Check-up Questions 01

Q1 Translate the sentence below into Korean.

Global Business English refers to English used for the conduct of global business and international trade or global business transactions.

➡

Q2 Write the following sentence in English.

비즈니스는 물품 및 서비스에 대한 생산, 유통, 매매 또는 매입을 통한 수익 창출 또는 금전적 이윤의 추구를 목적으로 정기적으로 행해지는 모든 인간의 활동을 칭한다.

[Useful expressions]

- refer to~: ~을 칭하다
- undertake: ~을 행하다
- on a regular basis: 정기적으로
- with object to 〈Verb〉: ~하는 것을 목적으로

➡

Q3 Which one is NOT considered a characteristic of business?

① Regular deals in goods and services
② Temporary exchange of goods and services
③ Requirement for investment
④ Aims at earning profit

Q4 What is NOT in the scope of Global Business English in this book?

① Business writings and correspondence
② Business transactions and their phases
③ Business consultation and domestic business law
④ Business expressions for market research, presentations, meetings, etc.

2

CHAPTER

Global Business English

The Incoterms® Rules 2020

Chapter

2 The Incoterms® Rules 2020

Key Sentences

Trade terms are a set of uniform rules codifying the interpretation of trade terms defining the price composition and the rights and obligations of the buyer and the seller in global business transactions.

Objectives

After studying this lesson, you will be able to:

- understand the definition and role of international trade terms
- define Incoterms® 2020
- identify 11 trade rules

2-1 Definition and the Role of International Trade Terms and Practices

국제무역조건 및 관행의 정의와 역할

국제무역조건은 비즈니스 거래 또는 무역 관행에서 세계적으로 인정되는 일련의 국제규칙 및 관습으로서 구매자와 판매자 간의 무역계약의 책임과 의무를 정의한다.

1. Incoterms의 목적과 범위

계약당사자는 각 국가 간의 상이한 무역관행을 인식하지 못하고 있다. 이로 인하여

시간 및 금전상의 낭비를 초래하는 오해, 분쟁 및 법정소송이 야기될 수 있다. 이러한 문제를 해소하기 위하여 국제상업회의소는 1936년에 거래조건의 해석에 관한 일련의 국제규칙을 출판하였다. 이 규칙을 "Incoterms 1936"이라고 한다.
그 후 이 규칙은 현재의 국제무역 관행과 일치시키기 위해 1953년, 1967년, 1976년, 1980년, 1990년, 2000년, 2011년에 개정이 이루어졌으며 현행 버전은 2019년 개정 후 2020년 1월 1일부터 시행되고 있다.

Incoterms의 목적과 적용 범위는 다음과 같다.

① 외국무역에 가장 일반적으로 사용되는 정형거래조건의 해석에 관하여 일련의 국제규칙을 제공하는 것이다.
② Incoterms의 범위는 매각된 물품("유형물"을 의미하고, 컴퓨터 소프트웨어와 같은 "무형물"은 포함하지 않는다)의 인도에 관하여 매매계약 당사자의 권리와 의무에 관련된 사항에 한정되어 있다.
③ 매매계약이 아니라 오히려 운송계약에 적용되는 것으로 오해받고 있다.
④ 당사자가 매매계약에 포함시키고자 하는 모든 의무를 규정하고 있는 것으로 잘못 추측되고 있다.
⑤ 매매계약하에서 매도인과 매수인 간의 관계만을 취급한다.
⑥ 수출입을 위한 물품의 통관의무, 물품의 포장, 인도를 받아야 하는 매수인의 의무 및 각각의 의무가 정당하게 이행되었다는 증거를 제공할 의무를 규정한다.
⑦ 매매계약의 이행에 있어서 소유권 및 기타 재산권의 이전, 계약위반 및 그 위반에 따른 결과, 그리고 특정 상황에서의 책임의 면제와 같이, 그러한 계약에서 일어나는 수많은 문제는 전혀 취급하지 않는다.
⑧ 계약위반의 결과와 여러 가지 장애에 의한 책임의 면제를 규정하지 않는다.
⑨ 실제적으로 단순히 국내시장 내의 물품매매계약에도 사용할 수 있다.

2. Incoterms 2020의 구조

(1) 2그룹 11개의 거래규칙

Incoterms 2020은 모두 11개의 거래규칙으로 구성되어 있으며, Incoterms 2010과 마찬가지로 운송수단의 사용 형태에 따라 2개의 명확한 그룹으로 구분하였다.

즉, 복합운송을 포함한 모든 형태의 운송수단에 사용될 수 있는 규칙과 오로지 해상 및 내수로 운송에만 사용될 수 있는 규칙으로 분류하고, 각 거래규칙별로 당사자의 의무조항도 마찬가지로 10개의 표제로 상호 대칭되게 기술하였다. 다만 의무사항의 순서에 있어서 변화가 있다.

표 2-1 Incoterms 2020 규칙의 구분

The 11 Incoterms 2020 rules are presented in two distinct classes	
복합운송을 포함한 모든 형태의 운송에 사용되는 규칙	해상 및 내수로 운송에만 사용되는 규칙
EXW(EX WORKS) FCA(FREE CARRIER) CPT(CARRIAGE PAID TO) CIP(CARRIAGE AND INSURANCE PAID TO) DAP(DELIVERED AT PLACE) DPU(DELIVERED AT PLACE UNPAID) DDP(DELIVERED DUTY PAID)	FAS(FREE ALONGSIDE SHIP) FOB(FREE ON BOARD) CFR(COST AND FREIGHT) CIF(COST INSURANCE AND FREIGHT)

(2) 매매당사자 간의 의무규정

개정 Incoterms 2020 규칙은 매매당사자 간의 의무사항을 동시에 비교하도록 편제를 바꾸어 사용자가 비용이나 의무사항을 쉽게 확인할 수 있다.

표 2-2 Incoterms 2020 규칙의 당사자 의무규정

A. 매도인의 의무	B. 매수인의 의무
A1. General obligations	B1. General obligations
A2. Delivery	B2. Taking delivery
A3. Transfer of risks	B3. Transfer of risks
A4. Carriage	B4. Carriage
A5. Insurance	B5. Insurance
A6. Delivery/transport document	B6. Proof of delivery
A7. Export/Import clearance	B7. Export/Import clearance
A8. Checking/packaging/marking	B8. Checking/packaging/marking
A9. Allocation of costs	B9. Allocation of costs
A10. Notice	B10. Notice

의무사항에 대한 수평적 체제(horizontal format)의 도입은 당사자들이 적절한 거래 조건을 선택하는 데 매우 유용하다. 또한 의무사항의 순서에도 변화를 주어 실제 거래 당사자들의 계약체결과 관련하여 중요도에 따라 새롭게 변경하였다. A1/B1 일반 의무인 물품제공/대금지급의무에 바로 이어 A2/B2 인도/인도의 수령, A3/B3 위험이전을 규정하여 사용자 입장에서 중요성에 따라 의무사항을 개편하였다.

International trade terms are a globally recognised set of international rules and conventions in business transactions or trade practices. They define trade contract responsibilities and liabilities between the buyer and the seller. They are invaluable and a cost saving tool. The exporter and the importer need not undergo lengthy negotiations about the conditions of each transaction. Once they have agreed, using a commercial term like FOB, they can sell and buy at FOB(Free On Board) without additional discussion on who will be responsible for the freight, cargo insurance, and other costs and risks.

When quoting prices to his/her overseas buyer, an exporter will naturally take into account payment of the various expenses involved in getting the goods from the factory or warehouse in his/her own country to the buyer's premises. In international trade or GBT, the basic terms and conditions should be clearly and reasonably stated in the contracts so as to clarify the duties and obligations of the Seller and the Buyer as follows.

- Terms of Quality
- Terms of Quantity
- Terms of Price
- Terms of Payment
- Terms of Shipment
- Terms of Insurance
- Terms of Packing
- Terms of Claim, Arbitration

Above all, the price terms are the most important one. For instance, an exporter, in calculating his/her export price, works out dock charges, clearing and forwarding charges, freight and insurance, and certainly also their profit margin, and adds them to the price paid to the manufacturer to make it, say, USD 1000 per metric ton CIF (Cost, Insurance and Freight) New York including 5% commission. Here, "USD 1000 per metric ton CIF New York including 5% commission" is one of the trade terms, or delivery terms as we normally call them.

Trade terms, also known as price terms or delivery terms, are a set of uniform rules codifying the interpretation of trade terms defining the price composition and the rights and obligations of the buyer and the seller in global business transactions. Trade terms are key elements of an international contract of sale, since they tell the parties what to do with respect to.

i) **Delivery Terms**: Carriage of the goods from the seller to the buyer and division of costs and risks between the parties.

ii) **Price Terms**: Stipulating what are included in the price the buyer paid to the seller, e.g. cost, freight, insurance, export and import clearance fees, etc.

iii) **Delivery Obligations**: What documents should the seller provide, e.g. bill of lading(B/L), insurance policy, inspection certificate, etc.

Trade terms are standardised terms used in sales contracts that describes the place and means of transfer of goods from the seller and the buyer. These trade terms, such as FOB and cost, insurance, and the price, identify the time when the risk of loss shifts from the seller to the buyer, and when the costs of freight and insurance divide. The use of trade terms greatly simplifies the process of negotiation of the contract, thus saving time and costs for business transactions.

2-2 Introduction to Incoterms® 2020

1. The purpose of the text of this Introduction is fourfold

- To explain what the Incoterms 2020 rules do and do NOT do and how they are best incorporated;
- To set out the important fundamentals of the Incoterms rules: the basic roles and responsibilities of seller and buyer, delivery, risk, and the relationship between the Incoterms rules and the contracts surrounding a typical contract of sale for export/import and also, where appropriate, for domestic sales;
- To explain how best to choose the right Incoterms rule for the particular sale contract; and
- To set out the central changes between Incoterms® 2010 and Incoterms 2020.

2. The Introduction follows this structure

I. What the Incoterms rules do

II. What the Incoterms rules do NOT do

III. How best to incorporate the Incoterms rules

IV. Delivery, risk and costs in the Incoterms 2020 rules

V. Incoterms 2020 rules and the carrier

VI. Rules for the contract of sale and their relationship to other contracts

VII. The eleven Incoterms® 2020 rules-"sea and inland waterway" and "any mode(s) of transport": getting it right

VIII. Order within the Incoterms 2020 rules

IX. Differences between Incoterms 2010 and Incoterms 2020

X. Caution with variants of Incoterms rules.

3. This Introduction gives guidance on the use of, and about the fundamental principles behind, the Incoterms 2020 rules.

4. The Incoterms rules explain a set of eleven of the most commonly-used three-letter trade terms, eg. CIF. DAP. etc., reflecting business-to- business practice in contracts for the sale and purchase of goods.

5. The Incoterms rules describe

- Obligations: Who does what as between seller and buyer, e.g. who organises carriage or insurance of the goods or who obtains shipping documents and export or import licences;
- Risk: Where and when the seller "delivers" the goods, in other words where risk transfers from seller to buyer; and
- Costs: Which party is responsible for which costs, for example transport, packaging, loading or unloading costs, and checking or security-related costs.

The Incoterms rules cover these areas in a set of ten articles, numbered A1/B1 etc., the A articles representing the seller's obligations and the B articles representing the buyer's obligations. See paragraph 53 below.

6. "The Incoterms" rules are NOT in themselves – and are therefore no substitute for a contract of sale. They are devised to reflect trade practice for no particular type of goods-and for any. They can be used as much for the trading of a bulk cargo of iron ore as for five containers of electronic equipment or ten pallets of airfreighted fresh flowers.

7. The Incoterms rules do NOT deal with the following matters

- whether there is a contract of sale at all;
- the specifications of the goods sold;
- the time, place, method or currency of payment of the price;

- the remedies which can be sought for breach of the contract of sale;
- most consequences of delay and other breaches in the performance of contractual obligations;
- the effect of sanctions;
- the imposition of tariffs;
- export or import prohibitions;
- force majeure or hardship:
- intellectual property rights; or
- the method, venue, or law of dispute resolution in case of such breach.

Perhaps most importantly, it must be stressed that the Incoterms rules do NOT deal with the transfer of property/title/ownership of the goods sold.

8. These are matters for which the parties need to make specific provision in their contract of sale. Failure to do so is likely to cause problems later if disputes arise about performance and breach. In essence, the Incoterms 2020 rules are not themselves a contract of sale: they only become part of that contract when they are incorporated into a contract which alreadyexists. Neither do the Incoterms rules provide the law applicable to the contract. There may be legal regimes which apply to the contract, whether international, like the Convention on the International Sale of Goods(CISG): or domestic mandatory law relating, for example, to health and safety or the environment.

2-3 Differences between Incoterms 2010 and 2020

1. The most important initiative behind the Incoterms 2020 rules has been to focus on how the presentation could be enhanced to steer users towards the right Incoterms rule for their sale contract. Thus:

a) a greater emphasis in this Introduction on making the right choice;
b) a clearer explanation of the demarcation and connection between the sale contract and its ancillary contracts;
c) upgraded Guidance Notes presented now as Explanatory Notes to each Incoterms rule; and
d) a re-ordering within the Incoterms rules giving delivery and risk more prominence.

All these changes, though cosmetic in appearance, are in reality substantial attempts on the part of ICC to assist the international trading community towards smoother export/import transactions.

2. Apart from these general changes, there are more substantive changes in the Incoterms 2020 rules when compared with Incoterms 2010. Before looking at those changes, mention must be made of a particular development in trade practice which occurred since 2010 and which ICC has decided should not lead to a change in the Incoterms 2020 rules. namely Verified Gross Mass (VGM).

3. Note on Verified Gross Mass(VGM)-Since 1 July 2016, Regulation 2 under the International Convention for the Safety of Life at Sea(SOLAS) imposed on shippers in the case of the shipment of containers the obligation either to weigh the packed container using calibrated and certified equipment, or to weigh the contents of the container and add the weight of the container when empty. In either case, the VGM is to be recorded with the carrier. A failure to comply bears the sanction under SOLAS Convention that the container should not be loaded onto a ser.

4. Returning to the changes made by ICC to the Incoterms 2010 rules in the Incoterms 2020 rules, these are

a) Bills of lading with an on-board notation and the FCA Incoterms rule

b) Costs, where they are listed

c) Different levels of insurance cover in CIF and CIP

d) Arranging for carriage with seller's or buyer's own means of transport in FCA, DAP, DPU and DDP

e) Change in the three-letter initials for DAT to DPU

f) Inclusion of security-related requirements within carriage obligations and costs

g) Explanatory Notes for Users

[Figure 2-1] Quick Reference for 11 Incoterms® 2020 Rules

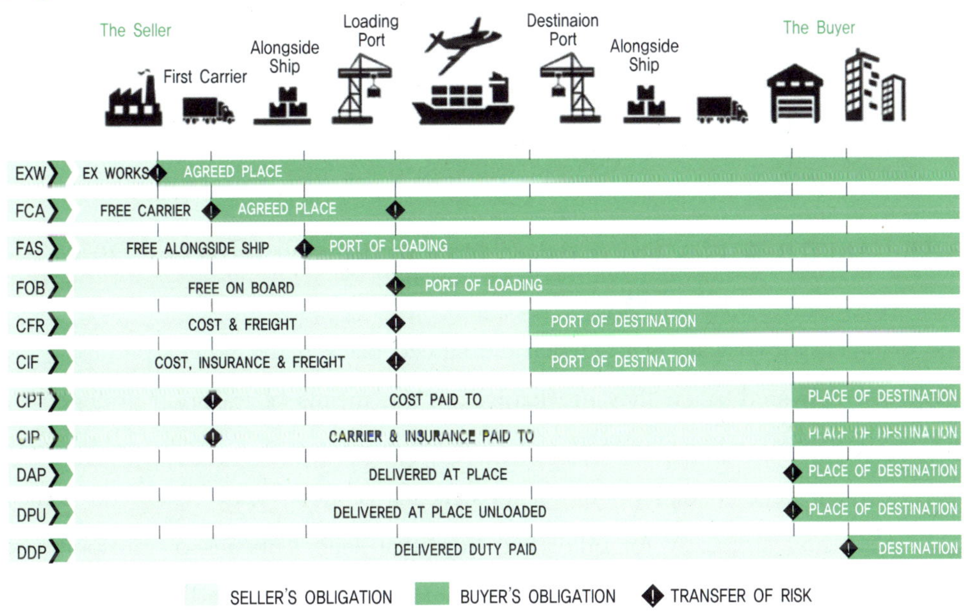

2-4 Incoterms® 2020 Rules

1. Rules for Any Mode or Modes of Transport

(1) EXW(공장인도)

EX WORKS ➲ EXW (insert named place of delivery) Incoterms® 2020

Ex Works means that the seller delivers the goods to the buyer when it places the goods at the disposal of the buyer at the named place (like a factory or warehouse), and that named place may or may not be the seller's premises. The seller does not need to load the goods on any collecting vehicle, nor does it need to clear the goods for export, where such clearance is applicable.

(2) FCA(운송인인도)

FREE CARRIER ➲ FCA (insert named place of delivery) Incoterms® 2020

Free Carrier (named place) means that the seller delivers the goods to the buyer in one or other of two ways. First, when the named place is the seller's premises, the goods are delivered when they are loaded on the means of transport arranged by the buyer. Second, when the named place is another place, the goods are delivered when, having been loaded on the seller's means of port, They reach the named other place and are ready for unloading from that seller's means of transport and at the disposal of the carrier or of another person nominated by the buyer.

Whichever of the two is chosen as the place of delivery, that place identifies where risk transfers to the buyer and the time from which costs are for the buyer's account.

(3) CPT(운송비지급인도)

CARRIAGE PAID TO ➲ CPT (<u>insert named place of destination</u>) Incoterms® 2020

Carriage Paid To means that the seller delivers the goods - and transfers the risk-to the buyer

- by handing them over to the carrier,
- contracted by the seller,
- or by procuring the goods so delivered.
- The seller may do so by giving the carrier physical possession of the goods in the manner and at the place appropriate to the means of transport used.

(4) CIP(운송비·보험료지급인도)

CARRIAGE AND INSURANCE PAID TO ➲ CIP (<u>insert named place of destination</u>) Incoterms® 2020

Carriage and Insurance Paid to means that the seller delivers the goods - and transfers the risk-to the buyer,

- by handing them over to the carrier,
- contracted by the seller,
- or by procuring the goods so delivered.

• The seller may do so by giving the carrier physical possession of the goods in the manner and at the place appropriate to the means of transport used.

carrier or another person nominated by the seller at an agreed place (if any such place is agreed between parties) and that the seller must contract for and pay the costs of carriage necessary to bring the goods to the named place of destination. The seller also contracts for insurance cover against the buyer's risk of loss of or damage to the goods during the carriage. The buyer should note that under CIP the seller is required to obtain insurance only on minimum cover. Should the buyer wish to have more insurance protection, it will need either to agree as much expressly with the seller or to make its own extra insurance arrangements.

(5) DAP(목적지인도)

DELIVERED AT PLACE ➲ DAP (insert named terminal at port or place of destination) Incoterms® 2020

Delivered at Place means that the seller delivers the goods – and transfers risk – to the buyer,

- when the goods are placed at the disposal of the buyer
- on the arriving means of transport ready for unloading
- at the named place of destination or
- at the agreed point within that place, if any such point is agreed.

The seller bears all risks involved in bringing the goods to the named place of destination or to the agreed point within that place. In this Incoterms rule, therfore, delivery and arrival at the destination are the same.

(6) DPU(도착지양하인도)

DELIVERED AT PLACE UNLOADED ➲ DPU (<u>insert named place of destination</u>) Incoterms® 2020

Delivered at Place Unloaded means that the seller delivers the goods – and transfers risk – to the buyer,

- when the goods once unloaded from the arriving means of transport,
- are placed at the disposal of the buyer
- at the agreed point within that place, if any such point is agreed.

The seller bears all risks involved in bringing the goods to and unloading them at the named place of destination. In this Incoterms rule, therefore, delivery and arrival at the destination are the same. DPU is the only Incoterms® rule that requires the seller to unload goods at destination.

(7) DDP(관세지급인도)

DELIVERED DUTY PAID ➲ DDP (<u>insert named place of destination</u>) Incoterms® 2020

Delivered Duty Paid means that the seller delivers the goods to the buyer,

- when the goods are placed at the disposal of the buyer
- cleared for import,
- on the arriving means of transport
- ready for unloading

• at the named place of destination or at the agreed point within that place, if any such point is agreed.

The seller bears all risks involved in bringing the goods to the named place of destination or to the agreed point within that place. In this Incoterms rule, therfore, delivery and arrival at the destination are the same.

when the goods are placed at the disposal of the buyer, cleared for import on the arriving means of transport ready for unloading at the named place of destination. The seller bears all the costs and risks involved in bringing the goods to the place of destination and has an obligation to clear the goods not only for export but also for import, to pay any duty for both export and import and to carry out all customs formalities.

2. Rules for Sea and Inland Waterway Transport

(1) FAS(선측인도)

FREE ALONGSIDE SHIP ➲ FAS (<u>insert named port of shipment</u>) Incoterms® 2020

Free Alongside Ship means that the seller delivers when the goods are placed alongside the vessel (e.g., on a quay or a barge) nominated by the buyer at the named port of shipment. The risk of loss of or damage to the goods passes when the goods are alongside the ship, and the buyer bears all costs from that moment onwards.

(2) FOB(본선인도)

FREE ON BOARD ➲ FOB (insert named port of shipment) Incoterms® 2020

Free On Board means that the seller delivers the goods on board the vessel nominated by the buyer at the named port of shipment or procures the goods already so delivered. The risk of loss of or damage to the goods passes when the goods are on board the vessel, and the buyer bears all costs from that moment onwards.

(3) CFR(운임포함인도)

COST AND FREIGHT ➲ CFR (insert named port of destination) Incoterms® 2020

Cost and Freight means that the seller delivers the goods on board the vessel or procures the goods already so delivered. The risk of loss of or damage to the goods passes when the goods are on board the vessel. The seller must contract for and pay the costs and freight necessary to bring the goods to the named port of destination.

(4) CIF(운임 · 보험료포함인도)

COST, INSURANCE AND FREIGHT ➲ CIF (insert named port of destination) Incoterms® 2020

Cost, Insurance and Freight means that the seller delivers the goods on board the vessel or procures the goods already so delivered. The risk of loss of or damage to the goods passes when the goods are on board the vessel. The seller must contract for and pay the costs and freight necessary to bring the goods to the named port of destination.

The seller also contracts for insurance cover against the buyer's risk of loss of or damage to the goods during the carriage. The buyer should note that under CIF the seller is required to obtain insurance only on minimum cover. Should the buyer wish to have more insurance protection, it will need either to agree as much expressly with the seller or to make its own extra insurance arrangements.

Key Expressions & Technical Terms

- **International Trade Terms:** International trade terms are a globally recognised set of international rules and conventions in business transactions or trade practices. They define trade contract responsibilities and liabilities between the buyer and the seller.

- **EXW(EX WORKS):** The seller just needs to prepare the goods for buyer in his/her premises or another named place like factory. The seller doesn't need to load the goods or prepare for the export clearance. When the buyer picks up the goods, he/she should bear all the risks and costs afterwards.

- **FCA(FREE CARRIER):** The seller needs to the deliver the goods to the carrier sent by the buyer and also prepare for the export clearance. When the seller deliver the goods to the carrier, the buyer bear all costs and risks. Carrier loads and unloads the goods.

- **CPT(CARRIAGE PAID TO):** The seller orders and paid a carrier to deliver the goods at a named place of shipment by the buyer, but the buyer should bear the risks after the goods are delivered to the carrier. Carrier loads and unloads the goods.

- **CIP(CARRIAGE AND INSURANCE PAID TO):** CIP is almost the same as CPT, except that the seller should procure minimum insurance coverage to the named place of shipment by buyer.

- **DAP(DELIVERED AT PLACE):** DAP is almost the same as DPU, except that the seller doesn't need to unload the good when arrival.

✔ **DPU(DELIVERED AT PLACE UNLOADED):** Delivered at Place Unloaded means that the seller delivers the goods – and transfers risk – to the buyer, when the goods once unloaded from the arriving means of transport.

✔ **DDP(DELIVERED DUTY PAID):** DDP is almost the same as DAP, except the seller should prepare for the import clearance and pay the import duty.

✔ **FAS(FREE ALONGSIED SHIP):** The seller should prepare for the export clearance and deliver the goods and place them alongside the vessel at the named port of shipment. The buyer bears all risks and costs afterwards.

✔ **FOB(FREE ON BOARD):** FOB is almost the same as FAS, except that the seller's responsibility is fulfilled till the goods are on board.

✔ **CFR(COST AND FREIGHT):** CFR is almost the same as FOB, except that the seller should paid for the freight cost (the buyer still bears the risks as that in terms of FOB).

✔ **CIF(COST, INSURANCE AND FREIGHT):** CIF is almost the same as CFR, except that the seller should procure minimum insurance coverage to the named place of shipment by buyer.

Check-up Questions 02

Q1 Translate the sentence below into Korean.

Trade terms are a set of uniform rules codifying the interpretation of trade terms defining the price composition and the rights and obligations of the buyer and the seller in global business transactions.

➥

Q2 What does Incoterms 2020 Rules DO?

➥

Q3 Compare the FCA/CPT/CIP with the Traditional FOB/CFR/CIF.

➥

Q4 What is trade terms?

➥

3

CHAPTER

Global Business English

Introduction to Global Business English

3-1 Definition of Global Business English

3-2 Differences between Business English and General English

3-3 Scope of Global Business English

3-4 Business Letter Layout

3-5 The Component Parts of Business Correspondence

Chapter

3 Introduction to Global Business English

Key Sentences

Global business English refers to English used for the conduct of global business and international trade or global business thansaction.

Objectives

After studying this lesson, you will be able to:

- define global business english
- understand difference between daily english and business english
- understand the scope of business english
- identify the four stages of effective business writing
- explain the objectives of business

3-1 Definition of Global Business English

비즈니스 영어란?

일반적으로 비즈니스 영어는 국제무역, 상업 및 금융에 특히 적합한 영어의 한 형태이다. 따라서 비즈니스 영어는 예를 들어 주로 업무 회의, 판매 프레젠테이션, 협상, 비즈니스 서신, 비즈니스 보고서, 요약 등에 일반적으로 사용되는 종류의 영어를 말한다.

Global Business English is basically defined as English used for the conduct of global business and international trade. It is generally taught to non-native English speakers who desire to do business with English speakers from around the world. Thus, it is purely a functional category of Business English aimed at preparing learners for effective communication in a global context. On the other hand, it can also be learned by native English speakers who are more familiar with casual use of the language and are not sure of their footing when it comes to formal, multi-national office environment conversations, and global business contracts or transactions.

According to The New Oxford Dictionary of English, business means a person's regular occupation, profession, or trade for a commercial house or firm. It also indicates the practice of making one's living by engaging in commerce(buying and selling). English, originally the language of England, is now widely spoken in many varieties throughout the world. Global Business English, therefore, is the Business English used in mercantile transactions worldwide.

3-2 Differences between Business English and General English

1. What Distinguishes Business English?*

English is the language of international business, and Business English can be defined as the use or application of English language skills as a global business communication tool. A general English course for business people is not the same as Business English. Likewise, it is not just about learning lots of business vocabulary. Of course, it does involve this, but it is a great deal more than just that. It is, in effect, all about the acquisition of an international communication skill-set, using the medium of the English language.

* http://keyenglish.ro/articles/how-is-business-english-different-from-general-english.html(2023.07.01)

Most people using Business English in the global workplace are non-native English speakers, from a variety of cultures, languages and nationalities, all using what has become, in effect, the 'national' language of planet Earth. Therefore, a very important aspect of Business English is that it is ***cross-cultural***; whereas language-learning normally involves acquiring some knowledge of the culture that the language represents, Business English by its very nature transcends cultures while at the same time respecting them. A good Business English trainer will have an acute awareness of this, and will adapt the use of English to the trainee's culture rather than the other way around.

There are a number of other important differences between Business English and general English.

- Business English is not so much about learning 'to speak a new language' as it is about learning to use the language we already know, in a practical business and professional context
- Business English is not just about using a second or foreign language; many of the skills used are also skills that are required to be learned by native-speakers
- In a general English group, all the learners should be at the same level. While useful, this is not always necessary in Business English, because the focus is on acquiring specific communication skills which can have application at different levels (it does, however, assume that all trainees are at a given minimum level - and they should not be too far apart)
- Time is a more important factor: the business English trainee must acquire a given set of language-based skills quickly, and does not have the time for prolonged courses that more often than not include skills that he will never need or use
- While various teaching approaches and methodologies can apply in general English learning, the approach in Business English is essentially a task-based one, i.e. *Learning-by-doing.* The learner is given a specific task as an exercise,

e.g. write an email with a given objective in mind, in which he has the opportunity to apply his new English skills in a practical way.

3-3 Scope of Global Business English

The focus in Business English is on the language and skills required for regular business communication: the vocabulary of trade, business contracts and transactions, presentations, negotiations, meetings, daily conversations, networking, correspondence and report writing, etc. The strict rules of grammar are sometimes ignored or sidestepped for these purposes. G.B. Hotchkiss & Kilduff, in one of their books, said "Business English includes all written messages in English that are used in transactions."

Business English varies depending on different aspects to different people. For some, it focuses on vocabulary and topics regarding trade, business contracts, finance and international relations. For others, it means the communication skills used in the workplace, and focuses on the language and skills necessary for typical business communication such as presentations, negotiations, meetings, socialising, correspondence, report writing, and so on.

3-4 Business Letter Layout

비즈니스 레터에는 블록 스타일, 수정된 블록 스타일, 세미 블록 스타일의 세 가지 주요 스타일이 있다. 각각은 동일한 정보를 포함하여 거의 동일한 방식으로 작성되지만 레이아웃은 각각 약간씩 다르다.

1. Layout of the Business Letter

Business letter layout is important. There are three main layouts that are commonly used and people will be used to seeing them when they receive business letters.

LETTERHEAD

Date ____________________

Reference ________________

Inside Address ___________

____

____

Attention ________________

Salutation _______________

Subject _________________

Body of the Letter____

____

____

____

____

Complimentary Close

COMPANY'S NAME ______________

(Writer's Signature) ______________

Writer's Typed Name ____________

Title __________________________

Typist's Initials _________________

Enclosures

C.C.

P.S.

(1) Full Block Style

When writing business letters, you must pay special attention to the style and font used. The most common layout of a business letter is known as full block style. Using this style, the entire letter is left justified and single spaced except for a double space between paragraphs.

(2) Modified Block

Another widely utilized format is known as modified block style. In this type, the body of the letter and the sender's and recipient's addresses are left justified and single-spaced. However, for the date and closing, tab to the center point and begin to type.

(3) Semi-Block

The final, and least used, style is semi-block. It is much like the modified block style except that each paragraph is indented instead of left justified.
Keep in mind that different organizations have different format requirements for their professional communication. While the examples provided by the OWL contain common elements for the basic business letter(genre expectations), the format of your business letter may need to be flexible to reflect variables like letterheads and templates. Our examples are merely guides.

If your computer is equipped with Microsoft Office 2000, the Letter Wizard can be used to take much of the guesswork out of formatting business letters. To access the Letter Wizard, click on the Tools menu and then choose Letter Wizard. The Wizard will present the three styles mentioned here and input the date, sender address and recipient address into the selected format. Letter Wizard should only be used if you have a basic understand of how to write a business letter. Its templates are not applicable in every setting. Therefore, you should consult a business writing handbook if you have any questions or doubt the accuracy of the Letter Wizard.

3-5 The Component Parts of Business Correspondence

일반적인 비즈니스 서신은 서두, 날짜, 내부 주소, 인사말, 본문, 결미 인사 및 서명의 7개 부분으로 구성된다.
이런저런 이유로 비즈니스 서신에 더 많은 부분을 포함해야 할 수 있다. 예를 들어 특정인의 이름을 알지 못한 채 특정인에게 보내는 서신을 보내야 할 때, 이 섹션에 나열된 부분 중 하나 또는 모두를 편지에 추가할 수 있다.

1. The Essential Parts of a Business Letter

A typical business letter consists of seven parts: the letterhead, the date line, the inside address, the salutation, the body of letter, the complimentary close, and the signature.

(1) The Letterhead

The letterhead is the heading at the top of a letter. It usually consists of the name, address, telephone number and fax number of a company. The letterhead can be typed out but is usually printed on the company's stationery(such stationery is also called letterhead). In addition, the printed letterhead may also include other items such as the company logo, web site, e-mail address, etc. The following is a sample letter(block form) containing all the essential parts.

PNU Cosmetic Co., Inc.

63-2, Busandaehag-ro, Geumjeong-gu, Busan, 46241, Korea

Tel: +82-51-123-5678, Fax: +82-51-123-4567

E-mail: ekcostmetic@kornet.net

(2) The Date Line

The format of the date line differs from country to country. The common ones are M/D/Y(typical American), D/M/Y(typical British). While we Korean prefer Y/M/D format, it is better to use M/D/Y or D/M/Y format in English letters. The month written in letters is preferred because figures may create confusion.

American Style: March 7, 2022.
British Style: 7th March, 2022.

(3) The Inside Address

The inside address is the recipient's address, identical to the delivery address on the envelope. In Korean letters, there is no inside address except where a windowed envelop is used. In this case, the inside address serves as the delivery address.

Mr. John F Dolan, President
America International Co., Inc.
350 Fifth Avenue, West
New York, NY 10018, U.S.A.

(4) The Salutation

The salutation is the greeting to your recipient. It usually includes a personal or professional title and the name of the recipient. The salutation varies according to the writer-recipient relationship and the formality level of the letter. The following table shows some common salutations.

Salutation	People to Address
Dear Mr. XXX	men
Dear Mrs. XXX	married women
Dear Miss XXX	unmarried women and girls
Dear Ms. XXX	women, marital status unknown
Dear Dr. XXX	physicians, Ph.D. holders
Dear Prof. XXX	professors and any holder of a professorial rank
Dear Sir(s)	no specific reference, formal
Gentlemen	no specific reference, formal
Ladies and Gentlemen	no specific reference, formal
To Whom It May Concern	You don't know yet who is the recipient
(Dear) First name only	close friend, informal

(5) The Body of Letter

The body of the letter is the main and largest part of a letter. The body is made up of one or more paragraphs in which the main idea of the letter is relayed. The first paragraph of the body of a letter should include the reason for writing. Additional paragraphs should go into more detail about the subject. The last paragraph of the body should summarize the message and make any necessary clarifications. There is no requirement for how many paragraphs should make up the body of a letter.

The body follows the heading, date, address, salutation and subject line. The closing and signature follow the body.

(6) The Complimentary Close

This part is like bidding farewell to someone with a handshake, a pat on the shoulder, a wave of the hand, or a kiss. Like the salutation, the complimentary close has some variations in style: formal, semiformal and informal. And this style shall match that of the salutation. The closing begins at the same vertical point as your date and one line after the last body paragraph. Capitalize the first word only (for example: Thank you) and leave four lines between the closing and the sender's name for a signature. If a colon follows the salutation, a comma should follow the closing; otherwise, there is no punctuation after the closing. Below are some samples of the complimentary close.

American Style	British Style
Yours truly	Yours faithfully
Yours very truly	Yours very faithfully
Truly yours	Faithfully yours
Very truly yours	Very faithfully yours

(7) The Signature

The signature(sometimes called the signature block) consists of a symbol (handwritten or chopped, usually illegible), the typed-out name(so that you know who signs it), and a title.

Complimentary Close
COMPANY'S NAME
(Writer's Signature)
Writer's Typed Name
Title

2. The Optional Parts of a Business Letter

For one reason or another, you may need more parts to be included in a business letter, say to direct the letter to a specific person without your knowing the name of that person. Any one or all the parts listed in this section can be added to the letter.

(1) Reference No. or File No.

Reference No. is a unique number on an order, application, etc, used to designate and quickly locate that order, application, etc.

	Date line
	Our Reference No.
Inside Address	

(2) The Attention Line

If you want your letter attended by or directed to a specific person or department, add an attention line. This will speed up the sorting process within a company. The following is a sample letter(indented form) containing optional parts.

> Attention: Mr. Albert Wilson
> Attention: Purchasing Department
> Attention: Mr. Albert Wilson, Purchasing Department

(3) The Subject Line

The subject line helps both the sender and the recipient identify the subject matter. Below are some samples of the subject line.

> SUBJECT: EXTENSION OF L/C NO. 535
> Subject: Your Order No. 15
> Sub.: Hand Tools

(4) The Typist's Initials(Identification Marks)

The typist's initials are the initials of the writer and the typist. Typist initials are used to indicate the person who typed the letter. If you typed the letter yourself, omit the typist initials. Many businesses prefer to drop the typist's initials.

dictator: Albert Wilson typist: Alice Smith
AW/as(dictator, typist)
AW-as(dictator, typist)
AW:as(dictator, typist)
AW:5(dictator, typist)

(5) The Enclosure Notation

When something else is sent together with the letter, you add the enclosure notation to inform the reader what is enclosed. If you have enclosed any documents along with the letter, such as a resume, you indicate this simply by typing Enclosures one line below the closing. For example:

Enclosure(Encl.: Enc.): One copy of Offer Sheet
Enc. (4): Packing List
Commodity Inspection Certificate
Insurance Policy
Sales Confirmation

(6) Carbon Copy Notation

Before the invention of the photocopier, carbon paper was used to create duplicates of documents by placing it between the original document and a blank piece of paper so that an image of the original was transferred to the blank piece of paper as a document was written or typed. A notation was placed at the bottom of the original document indicating for whom a "carbon copy" was created. This notation was typed, for example, as follows.

cc: John Smith

C.C.: America International Co., Inc.
Messrs. John & Co., Ltd.
Copies to: America International Co., Inc.
Messrs. John & Co., Ltd.

(7) The Postscript Notation

The postscript(often shortened into P.S.) is used to add an afterthought. In sales letters, it is used mainly as added punch.

P.S. Under a separate cover we are sending you the offer sheet and samples.
P.S. The enclosed postcard is for your convenience. Mail it today

(8) The Second Page Heading

When a letter runs more than one page long, the second page heading is necessary for quick identification. Always print the subsequent page(s) on plain paper (without letterhead). The following two examples are the most common.

Ms. Helen E. Mann 2 Mar. 10, 2022

Ms. Helen E. Mann
Mar. 10, 2022
Page 2

(9) Addressing of Envelopes

① Sender: Yang Kee Mulsan Co., Ltd., C.P.O. Box 125, 314-79, Daeyeon-dong, Nam-gu, Busan, (48434), Korea	Stamp ② VIA AIR MAIL
   ④ Attn: Mr. E.C. Black	③ Recipient: Pacific Coast Railways, Inc. 2561 California Avenue Seattle, WA 96514, U.S.A.

Key Expressions & Technical Terms

- ✔ **Business Correspondence**: The exchange of information in a written format for the process of business activities. Business correspondence can take place between organizations, within organizations or between the customers and the organization. The correspondence is generally of widely accepted formats that are followed universally.
- ✔ **The essential parts of a Business Letter**: It includes letterhead, inside address, salutation, complimentary close, body of letter, date line, and the signature. They are indispensable for Business Letter.
- ✔ **Letterhead**: The heading at the top of a letter. It consists of the name, address, telephone number and fax number of a company.
- ✔ **Salutation**: The greeting to one's recipient. It usually includes a personal or professional title and the name of the recipient.
- ✔ **Complimentary Close**: It is like bidding farewell to someone on the business letter. But it shows also your respect to your recipient.
- ✔ **Signature**: a symbol (handwritten or chopped, usually illegible), the writer's name and a title.
- ✔ **Attention Line**: A line of text after the address on a piece of correspondence, directing it to a particular person or department.
- ✔ **Carbon Copy Notation**: The under-copy of a document created when carbon paper is placed between the original and the under-copy during the production of a document. (the abbreviation cc) It indicate for whom a carbon copy was created.
- ✔ **Enclosure Notation**: when something else is sent together with the letter, add the enclosure notation to inform the reader what is enclosed.

Check-up Questions 03

Q1 Translate the sentence below into Korean.

Understanding the types of global business and how to write effective business correspondence is a prerequisite for mastering Global Business English.

➡

Q2 Write down the seven different types of global business or international trade in both English and Korean.

➡

Q3 What is NOT included in the 7C's for effective communication criteria?

① Clarity ② Conciseness
③ Correctness ④ Creativeness

Q4 Which one is NOT an essential part of a Business Letter?

① Letterhead ② Inside Address
③ Body of Letter ④ Postscript

Q5 What is the optional part of a Business Letter?

① Salutation
② Complimentary Close
③ Enclosure Notation
④ Signature

4 CHAPTER

Global Business English

Requisites for Global Business Transactions Key Sentences

Chapter

4 Requisites for Global Business Transactions Key Sentences

Key Sentences

Understanding the processes involved, parties participating, information exchanged and the rules that govern these exchanges is a requisite for the conduct of Global Business Transactions in four phases, i.e. Information, Agreement, Implementation and Follow-up phases.

Objectives

After studying this lesson, you will be able to:
- understand the Buy-Ship-Pay Model
- identify four phases of global business transactions(GBT)

4-1 The Buy-Ship-Pay Model(BSP)

Buy-Ship-Pay 비즈니스 프로세스 참조 모델은 국제 공급망과 관련된 주요 상업, 물류, 규제 및 지불절차를 식별하고 다양한 단계에서 당사자 간에 교환되는 정보에 대한 개요를 제공한다. 이 모델은 UN/CEFACT 모델링 방법론(UMM)에 따라 공식적으로 개발되었으며 국제 공급망 참조 모델로도 알려져 있다.

A supply chain embraces all activities necessary for goods to be produced and delivered to the final consumer. Such activities encompass sourcing of raw materials, preparing for transportation, requesting an import license, preparing documentation for Customs clearance, payment, and delivery to the customer. As a minimum, a supply chain involves two parties, the seller and the buyer. In reality, a supply chain involves many different parties. There can be private-sector traders, transport operators, service intermediaries, or regulatory bodies from the public sector. Adopting a supply chain perspective makes it possible to view and understand all possible processes and the inter-linkages between them. It provides the framework to logically connect different people, procedural phases and requirements in one picture of the global business transaction environment.

There are many variants of supply chains. Using a supply chain perspective therefore requires the use of a theoretical pattern that simplifies its complexity and can be used as a reference model. The *Buy-Ship-Pay Model(BSP)* developed by UN/CEFACT is an example of such a model. It presents the supply chain as a sequence of business processes that can be grouped into the high-level domains of Buy, Ship and Pay. Figure 4–1 below illustrates the use of the BSP approach. For each domain, the model presents key activities, such as the activity "insure cargo" for the step "prepare for export" of the Ship domain. The model can be used in various ways, for example to gain understanding of the processes and people involved, and to help identify the phases of given global business transactions (GBT).

[Figure 4–1] The UN/CEFACT Buy–Ship–Pay Model(BSP)

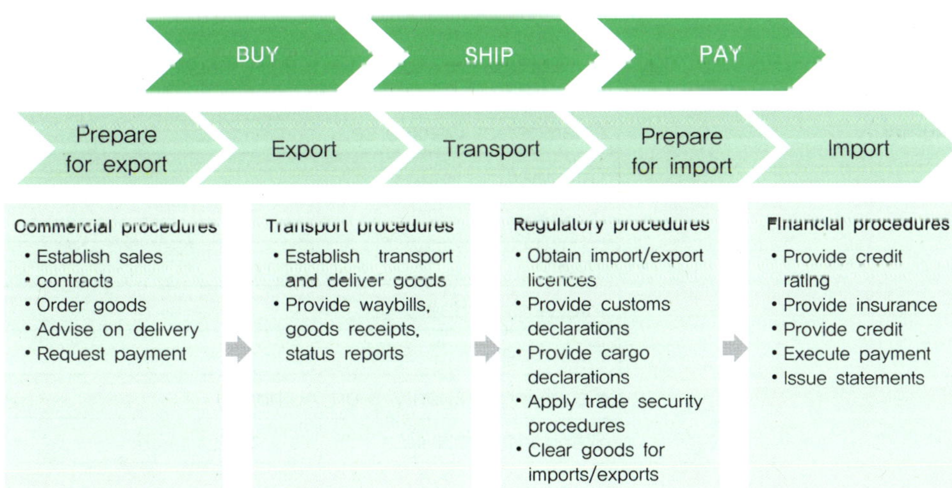

The Buy-Ship-Pay Model(BSP) developed by UN/CEFACT describes the main processes and parties in the global supply chain. The supply chain ensures the goods are ordered, shipped and paid for while complying with regulatory requirements and supporting trade security(or supply chain security). The BSP model identifies the key commercial, logistical, regulatory and payment procedures, involved in the global supply chain and provides an overview of the information exchanged between the parties throughout its various phases.

The BSP model identifies four main business partner types: Customer, Supplier, Intermediary and Authority. The types or organisations that make up these categories, and the roles they play, are introduced below.

Actor Types	Possible Actors & Roles
Customer	Buyer
	Consignee
	Payor
	Importer
	Ship to
Supplier	Consignor
	Payee
	Seller
	Manufacturer
	Exporter
	Ship from
Authority	Chamber of Commerce
	Consular
	Customs
	Health
	Intervention Board (EU)
	Licensing
	Receiving Authority (Port Authority)
	Standards Institute

Intermediary	Bank / Financial Institution
	Broker
	Carrier
	Credit Checking Company
	Credit insurer
	Commission Agent
	Export Agent
	Freight forwarder
	Import Agent
	Insurer
	Inspection company
	Receiving authority

i) Customer: A party who acquires, by way of trade, goods or services, and requires knowledge of sources of supply, best products/services at the best prices, simpler procedures, reduced restraints and minimum costs of operation.

ii) Supplier: A party who provides, by way of trade, goods or services, and aims to acquire increased market share, optimum profit, reduced restrictions to market, simpler procedures, reduced documentation and guaranteed payment.

iii) Authority: A statutory body existing within a jurisdiction and a specific area of responsibility that administers legislation to regulate trade and/or monitors compliance with existing legislation, and ensures that regulations are enforceable easily/effectively to protect the consumer from risk or protect the economy.

iv) Intermediary: A commercial party who provides services to Customers, Suppliers or Authorities within the global supply chain, and provides efficient procedures with a minimum of imposed restrictions/delays.

The following figure 4-2 illustrates the business processes and transactions that are included in the BSP model. Only the SHIP part is shown for the two top levels. Below that level, business process views of the named transactions are stored in the model. The diagram below shows the level of details of information available for each process.

[Figure 4-2] Business Processes and Transactions included in the BSP Model

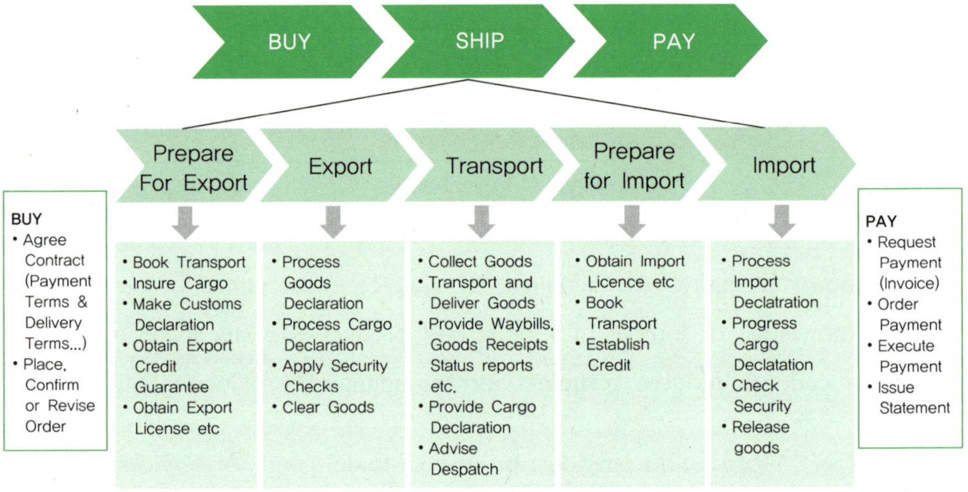

4-2 Four Phases of Global Business Transactions(GBT)

> GBT(Global Business Transactions)에 대한 BSP 모델은 정보단계, 계약단계, 이행단계 및 후속단계의 네 가지 주요 절차단계로 분류할 수 있다.

The BSP model for the Global Business Transactions(GBT) described above may be classified into four main procedural phases, i.e. information phase, agreement phase, implementation phase and follow-up phase as shown below.

Classification	Information Phase	Agreement Phase	Implementation Phase	Follow-up Phase
Procurement /Sales	• Overseas Market Research • Identify Potential Trading artners	• Establish Business Agreement via Negotiation • Order	• Deliver. Pay Supplier • Provide or Despatch Advice • Provide Receipt Advice	• Provide Credit • Debit note
Logistics		Book Transport	• Transport Goods • Provide Status Reports • Pay for Logistics Services	
Financial Services	Credit Inquiry	• Request Credit • Request Insurance	• Provide Credit • Provide Insurance • Pay Financial Service Provider • Handle Payments	Claims & Dispute Settlement
Regulation	International Trade Terms	• Request Export Licence • Request Health Certificate	• Clear Goods for Import and Export • Pay Regulatory Charges	

[Figure 4-3] Four Phases of GBT and Major Activities

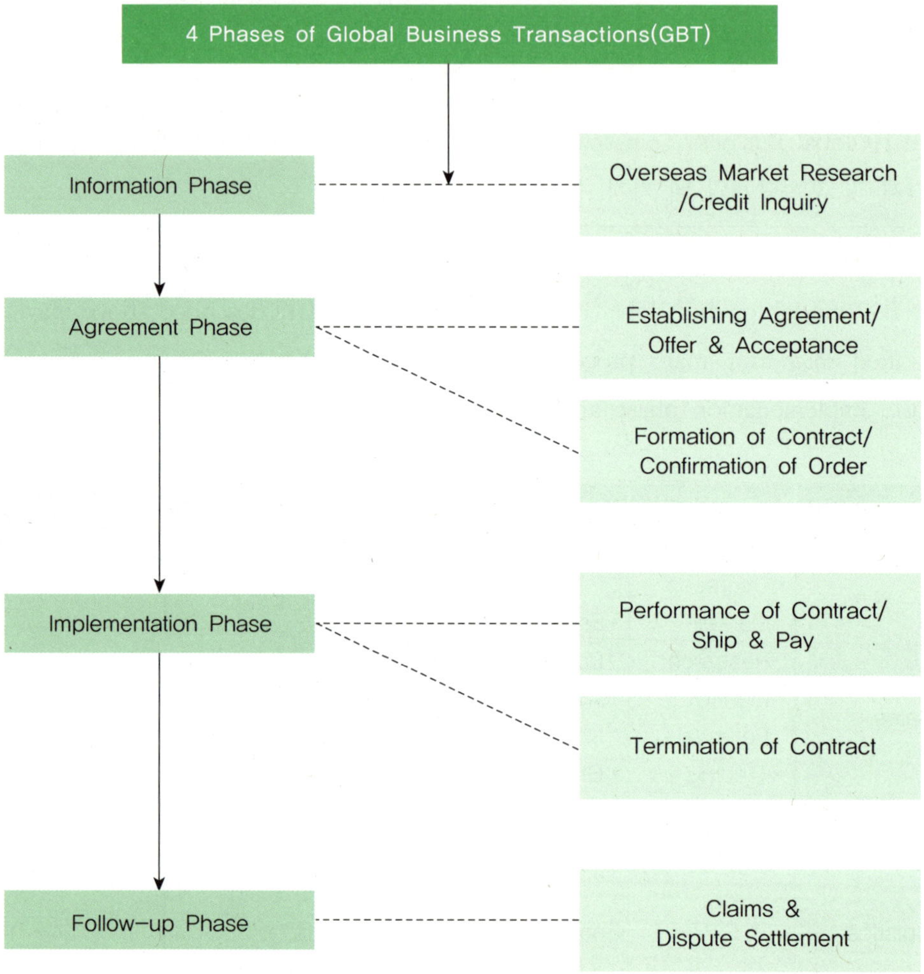

Key Expressions & Technical Terms

✔ **Buy-Ship-Pay Model**: The Buy-Ship-Pay model developed by UN/CEFACT describes the main processes and parties in the international supply chain. The Buy-Ship-Pay model identifies the key commercial, logistical, regulatory and payment procedures involved in the international supply chain and provides an overview of the information exchanged between the parties throughout its various steps.

✔ **Consignee**: The consignee is the entity who is financially responsible(the buyer) for the receipt of a shipment.

✔ **Consignor**: The consignor, in a contract of carriage, is the person sending a shipment to be delivered whether by land, sea or air.

✔ **Freight Forwarder**: A person or company that organizes shipments for individuals or corporations to get goods from the manufacturer or producer to a market, customer or final point of distribution.

✔ **Information Phase**: Overseas market research, relevant information for potential business transactions and trading partners such as credit inquiry can be acknowledged. Business partners inform others about alternative partners for a transaction and their bids, prices, trade terms and further conditions.

✔ **Agreement Phase**: Negotiations between a supplier and a customer will be held during this phase. At best, it will end in a contract, which determines the rights and duties of the participating parties involved.

- ✔ **Implementation Phase**: The exchange of products itself and the according payment, logistics, insurance and customs services take place in this phase.

- ✔ **Follow-up Phase**: Claims by trading partners involved may occur and the dispute settlement procedure between the contracting parties will be determined at this phase.

Check-up Questions 04

Q1 Translate the paragraph below into Korean.

The Buy-Ship-Pay(BSP) model developed by UN/CEFACT describes the main processes and parties in the global supply chain. The supply chain ensures the goods are ordered, shipped and paid for while complying with regulatory requirements and supporting trade security. The BSP model identifies the key commercial, logistical, regulatory and payment procedures, involved in the global supply chain and provides an overview of the information exchanged between the parties throughout its various phases.

➥

Q2 The BSP model identifies four main business partner types: customer, supplier, intermediary and authority. These types are paired with possible people and their roles as below. Which is NOT correct?

① Customer: Buyer, Consignee, Payor, Ship to

② Supplier: Consignor, Payee, Seller, Ship from

③ Authority: Consular, Customs, Standards Institute

④ Intermediary: Chamber of Commerce, Licensing, Receiving Authority

Q3 What are the four phases of Global Business Transactions(GBT)? Briefly explain the major activities for each phase in both English and Korean.

➥

Q4 Translate the paragraph below into Korean.

Trade terms, also known as price terms or delivery terms, are a set of uniform rules codifying the interpretation of trade terms defining the price composition and the rights and obligations of the buyer and the seller in global business transactions. Trade terms are standardised terms used in sales contracts that describe the place and means of the transfer of goods from the seller to the buyer. These terms, such as free on board(FOB) and cost, insurance, and the price, identify the time when the risk of loss shifts from the seller to the buyer, and the costs of freight and insurance. The use of trade terms greatly simplifies the process of negotiation of the contract, thus saving time and cost for business transactions.

➥

Q5 Which one of the 11 Incoterms® 2020 rules below can ONLY be used for Sea and Inland Waterway Transport?

① FCA(Free Carrier)
② CIP(Carriage, and Insurance Paid to)
③ DAT(Delivered at Place)
④ CFR(Cost and Freight)

Q6 Translate the paragraph below into Korean.

Please quote your best prices CIF Busan for 500 each of these coats in medium and small sizes and let us know if you could ship them within a fortnight of receipt of order No. 47684.

➥

5 CHAPTER

Global Business English

Information Phase

5-1 Overseas Market Research

5-2 Preparation for Global Business Transactions

5-3 Identifying Overseas Business/Trading Partners

Chapter 5

Information Phase

Key Sentences

At the Information Phase, overseas market research and relevant information for potential business transactions and trading partners, can be acknowledged. Business partners inform themselves about alternative partners for a transaction and their bids, prices, trade terms and further conditions.

Objectives

After studying this lesson, you will be able to:
- understand the definition of overseas market research
- identify contents of preparation for Global Business Transactions
- Identify Overseas Business/Trading Partners

5-1 Overseas Market Research

해외시장조사(Overseas Market Research)란 무역거래자가 해외시장의 환경 및 동향을 조사하고 고객이 원하고 있는 바를 파악하여 무역거래의 증진을 목적으로 행하는 시장조사를 말한다. 다시 말하면 특정물품에 대한 판매 또는 구매가능성(selling or buying feasibility)을 조사하는 것이다.

수출자의 입장에서 해외시장을 개척하고 이를 확대하는 데 있어서 제일 먼저 고려하여야 할 문제가 곧 해외시장조사이다. 수출자는 해외시장조사를 통하여 어느 지역의 시장에서 어떠한 거래처를 대상으로 어느 시기에 자신이 취급하고 있는 물품을 가장 합리적인 가격으로 유통비용을 최소화하여 많은 물량을 판매할 수 있는가를 과학적으로 조사·연구·분석하여야 한다. 해외시장조사는 지역적인 격리성, 상관습 및 언어 등의 차이로 인하여 조사에 어려움이 많이 따른다. 따라서 조사자의 충실하고 정확한 조사자료가 목적시장 진출 여부와 성공적인 거래관계를 유지하기 위한 전제조건이 된다.

해외시장조사의 내용은 우선적으로 목적시장의 일반적인 환경조사를 한 다음 고객조사, 상품조사, 판매경로조사, 판매조사 등을 보다 구체적으로 실시하고 마지막으로 믿을 만한 거래처를 발굴하는 단계를 거치게 된다.

1. Definition

Overseas Market Research(OMR) basically helps to identify the market potential for the given product in a region which is outside the domestic area. With OMR, one can understand about the prevailing economic and political environment in the subject region, which influences the marketing strategy and plans to be adapted suitably. OMR may also help to understand consumer behaviour; his/her tastes, preferences, likes and dislikes, beliefs, and customs etc., which in turn will help the manufacturer or trader to develop or trade suitable products. Understanding the present competition scenario in the subject region is extremely important as well. In addition, we all know how important it is to understand government rules and regulations in the subject region/country, as this will decide the business prospectus at the very first stage. OMR may also give some guidelines as regards to selection of effective and efficient distribution channels.

2. 10 Ways to Do Overseas Market Research(OMR)

- *Do make sure you understand the marketplace and the customer's needs and wants yourself.* If necessary, let professional marketers that know your target market(s) research consumers and the marketplace first and develop structures to manage marketing information beforehand.
- *Do use the internet to search for free reports on your potential markets regularly.*

If necessary, let professional marketers do this preliminary research.

- *Do research your (potential) competitors thoroughly*. In many Western countries, for example, companies are open about their strategies and communicate about their markets and performance openly; so, think of the possibility of having professional marketers collect the information locally. It's a fast and inexpensive way to gain hands-on knowledge.
- *Do talk with your foreign customers openly about your plans if it does not harm their interests*. Customers often are a cheap and very reliable source for market information, especially if the relationship is strong.
- When the internet is a potential medium in marketing communications, *do use tools like Google Analytics*(http://www.google.com/analytics/) *to retrieve market information*.
- To make sure adequate internet marketing information is gathered, *do hire professional internet marketers with access to or actual native language abilities for your potential target markets*.
- *Do narrow the focus of any overseas market research*. Prepare for a dominating position in one market or part of a market before conquering the rest of the world.
- *Do make sure the outcome of your market research will enable you to make decisions on market segmentation and targeting and product differentiation and positioning*.
- *Do conduct any overseas market research with respect for – and in mind of the local culture*, – history and stage of development. Do not think light of prejudices.
- *Do get in touch with one or more of business/commerce organisations or authorities in the target market*. Send them an email, make a phone call, or contact them via their websites.

5-2 Preparation for Global Business Transactions

Once the overseas market research has been done and you've decided to sell (or buy) products abroad, you'll need to develop an export(or an import) plan. A crucial first step in planning is to develop broad consensus among key management personnel on the company's goals, objectives, capabilities, and constraints. In addition, since they will ultimately be responsible for its successful implementation and execution, the personnel involved in the exporting process should agree on all aspects of an export plan. The purposes of the export plan are (i) to assemble facts, constraints, and goals and (ii) to create an action statement that takes all of those elements into account. The plan includes specific objectives, sets forth time schedules for implementation, and marks milestones so that the degree of success can be measured and motivate personnel.

The following 10 questions should ultimately be addressed.

① Which products are selected for export development, and what modifications, if any, must be made to adapt them for overseas markets?

② Which countries are targeted for sales development?

③ In each country, what are the basic customer profiles, and what marketing and distribution channels should be used to reach customers?

④ What special challenges pertain to each market (e.g., competition, cultural differences, and import controls), and what strategy will be used to address them?

⑤ How will your product/s export sales price be determined?

⑥ What specific operational steps must be taken and when?

⑦ What will be the time frame for implementing each element of the plan?

⑧ What personnel and company resources will be dedicated to exporting?

⑨ What will be the cost in time and money for each element?

⑩ How will results be evaluated and used to modify the plan?

The first time an export plan is developed, it should be kept simple. It needs to be only a few pages long since important market data and planning elements may not yet be available. The initial planning efforts themselves gradually generate more information and insight. As you learn more about exporting and your company's competitive position, the export plan will become more detailed and complete.

From the start, your plan should be written and viewed as a flexible management tool, not as a static document. Objectives in the plan should be compared with actual results to measure the success of different strategies. Your company should not hesitate to modify the plan and make it more specific as new information and experience are gained. A detailed plan is recommended for companies that intend to export directly. Companies that choose indirect export methods may use much simpler plans. For more information on different approaches to exporting and their advantages and disadvantages, see below.

[Figure 5-1] Basic Concept of Business Environment(Transactions)

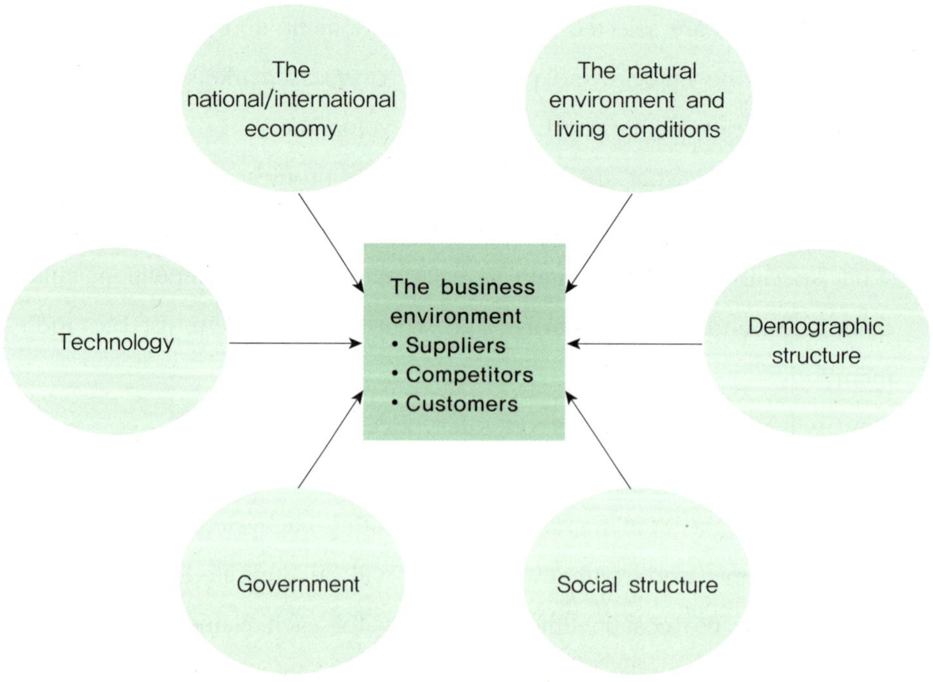

1. Methods and Channels of Export/Import

The most common methods of exporting are indirect selling and direct selling. In indirect selling, an export intermediary such as an export management company (EMC) or an export trading company(ETC) assumes responsibility for finding overseas buyers, shipping products, and getting paid. In direct selling, the home country producer deals directly with a foreign buyer. The paramount consideration in determining whether to market indirectly or directly is the level of resources your company is willing to devote to your global marketing effort. Other factors to consider when deciding whether to market indirectly or directly include the following.

- The size of your firm
- Tolerance for risk
- Resources available to develop the market
- Previous export experience and expertise
- Business conditions in the selected overseas markets

2. Approaches to Exporting/Importing

The way you choose to export your products can have a significant effect on your export plan and specific marketing strategies. The various approaches to exporting relate to your company's level of involvement in the export process.

ⅰ) Passively filling orders from domestic buyers, who then export the product. These sales are indistinguishable from other domestic sales as far as the original seller is concerned. Another party has decided that the product in question meets foreign demand. That party assumes all the risks and handles all the exporting details, in some cases even without the awareness of the original seller. (Many companies take a stronger interest in exporting when they discover that their product is already being sold overseas.)

ii) Seeking out domestic buyers who represent foreign end users or customers. Many domestic and foreign corporations, general contractors, foreign trading companies, foreign government agencies, foreign distributors, retailers, and others in Korea purchase for export. These buyers constitute a large market for a wide variety of goods and services. In this approach, your company may know that its product is being exported, but the domestic buyer still assumes the risk and handles the details of exporting.

iii) Exporting indirectly through intermediaries. With this approach, your company engages the services of an intermediary firm that is capable of finding foreign markets and buyers for your products. EMCs, STCs, global trade consultants, and other intermediaries can give you access to well-established expertise and business/trade contracts, but you retain considerable control over the process and can realise some of the other benefits of exporting, such as learning more about foreign competitors, new technologies, and other market opportunities.

iv) Export directly. This approach is the most ambitious and challenging because your company handles every aspect of the exporting process from market research and planning to foreign distribution and payment collections. A significant commitment of management time and attention is required to achieve good results. However, this approach may also be the best way to achieve maximum profits and long-term growth. With appropriate help and guidance from trade-related authorities, such as the Ministry of Trade, Industry & Energy(MOTIE) or Korea Trade-Investment Promotion Agency(KOTRA), freight forwarders, shipping companies, international banks, and others, even small or medium-sized firms can export directly. The exporting process today is easier and has fewer steps than ever before. For those who cannot make that commitment, the services of an EMC, ETC, trade consultant, or other qualified intermediary can be of great value.

Using an EMC or other intermediary, however, does not exclude the possibility of direct exporting for your firm. For example, your company may try to export directly to nearby markets such as China, Japan, or the Philippines, while letting an EMC handle more challenging sales to Egypt or France. You may also choose to gradually increase the level of direct exporting once you have gained enough experience and sales volume to justify added investment. Before making those kinds of decisions, you may want to consult trade specialists such as those at KOTRA, the Korea International Trade Association(KITA), or the Korea Trade Network(KTNET). They can be helpful in determining the best approach or mix of approaches for you and your company.

3. Distribution Considerations

Here are some points to consider when distributing your product.

- Which channels of distribution should your company use to market its products abroad?
- Where should your company produce its products, and how should it distribute them in the foreign market?
- What types of representatives, brokers, wholesalers, dealers, distributors, or end-use customers should you use?
- What are the characteristics and capabilities of the available intermediaries?
- Should you obtain the assistance of an EMC or an ETC?

4. Getting Organised for Exporting

A company new to exporting generally treats its export sales no differently from its domestic sales, using existing personnel and organisational structures. As international sales and inquiries increase, your company may choose to separate the management of its exports from that of its domestic sales. The advantages of separating international from domestic business include the centralisation of specialised skills needed to deal with international markets and the benefits of a focused marketing effort that is more likely to increase export sales. A possible disadvantage is that segmentation might be a less efficient use of company resources.

Your company can separate international from domestic business at different levels in the organisation. For example, when you first begin to export, you may create an export department with a full – or part – time manager who reports to the head of domestic sales and marketing. At a later stage, your company may choose to increase the autonomy of the export department to the point of creating an international division that reports directly to the president. Many smaller companies absorb export sales into existing functions; such an arrangement works effectively until export sales increase significantly. Regardless of how your company organises its exporting efforts, the key is to facilitate the marketer's job. Good marketing skills can help your firm operate in an unfamiliar market.

Experience has shown that a company's success in foreign markets depends less on the unique attributes of its products than on its marketing methods. Once your company is organised to handle exporting, a proper channel of distribution needs to be carefully chosen for each market. These channels include sales representatives, agents, distributors, retailers, and end users.

[Figure 5-2] Critical Flow of Export/Import Procedure by Global Enterprise

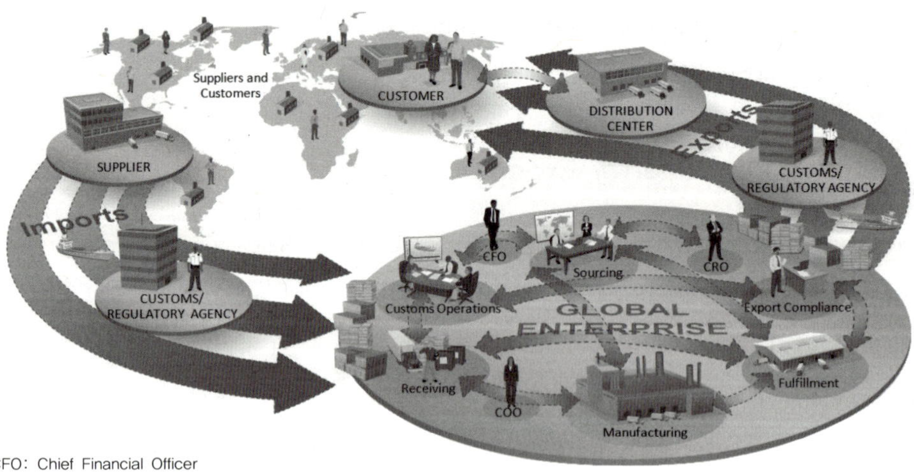

*CFO: Chief Financial Officer
**COO: Chief Operating Officer
***CRO: Chief Resource Officer

5-3 Identifying Overseas Business/Trading Partners

Finding the best possible overseas customers or partners is essential to the success of your company. Although many trading companies work on a "one-shot" deal basis, often the best way of achieving long-term success is by identifying and connecting with partners who will provide you with a steady stream of business. Such partners often come in the form of overseas agents or distributors.

There are a number of ways to identify prospective overseas partners or customers. The Korea Chamber of Commerce and Industry(KCCI) or KOTRA can help guide you through this process.

To select the best possible partner, a great deal of research and effort is required. Many trading companies and EMC start-ups are fortunate in that they already have existing partners in place(e.g., someone might want to start a trading company specialising in doing business with China because he/she might have family, friends or existing contacts there). If you do not have partners in place, however, you will need to do some extra ground work.

When you select a partner, you will want to make certain that your partner already has experience in your industry. For example, if you are selling high end women's skirts to the U.K., you will want to make sure that your partner already has experience in selling high-end apparel and has well-established sales channels into high-end apparel retailers in the U.K. Since you do not want to compete with your prospective partner's existing product line, you might want to make sure that the partner does not already carry high-end women's skirts, but perhaps other high-end items, such as women's jackets and trousers. In brief, you want to make sure that your partner will be a good "fit" with your needs, and toward this end, conduct careful research and investigation before making a final selection.

1. Request for introduction of overseas connections

[Model Letter 5-1: Request for introduction of overseas connections]

Gentlemen:

We are long-established exporters of all kinds of porcelain and have wide and close connections with the leading manufacturers here.

We are trying to extend our business to your market and shall be obliged if you will introduce us to some reliable firms in your city who are interested in handling porcelain.

As to our credit standing, The Hana Bank, Head Office, Seoul, will supply necessary information.

We thank you for your trouble in advance and look forward to an early reply form you.

Yours very truly

THE KOREA TRADING CO., LTD.

Jong-su Kim

Jong-su Kim

Export Manager

[주] Chamber of Commerce: 상업회의소, 단 한국 및 일본에서는 상공회의(Chamber of Commerce and Industry)/ The Secretary: 상공회의소 등의 단체에 사무적인 편지를 보낼 때는 반드시 "사무장" 앞으로 보내는 것이 관례로 되어 있다/ long-established: 창업한 지 오래된/ porcelain: 자기/ with and close connections: 넓고도 긴밀한 거래관계/ extend: 확장하다(=expand)/ shall be obliged if you will~: 해주시면 감사하겠습니다./ reliable firms: 신뢰할 수 있는 회사/ be interested in: ~에 관심이 있다/ handle: 취급하다/ as to: ~에 관해서는/ credit standing: 신용상태/trouble: 노고(수고)/ in advance: 미리/ look forward to: ~을 기대하다/ Export Manager: 수출부장

[Model Letter 5-2: Introduction of overseas connections]

Dear Sirs,

In compliance with your request of May 5, we are pleased to suggest the following firm:

Messers. H. Brown & W. Paker, Ltd.
18 Hill Street, London, W. 1. England.

While this concern is reliable and of good reputation here, we are unable to make ourselves responsible for them. For any information you may desire as to their standing, we advise you to write directly to them.

If there is anything further we can do for you, please do not hesitate to let us know.

Yours faithfully,

[주] in compliance with(=according to: in conformity to(with)): ~에 따라/ suggest the following firm(=recommend you~: introduce to you~): 회사를 추천한다/ concern: 회사(=firm company, corporation, house)/ be of good reputation: 평판이 좋다/ make oneself responsible for: ~의 책임을 지다/ please do not hesitate to do: 주저하지 않고 ~해 주세요.

2. Circular Letter

A letter that is sent to a usually big number of people is called a circular letter. The body of a circular letter may include information, instructions, or guidelines. A few examples of circular letters are official circulars, business circulars, miscellaneous circulars, and personal circulars. Business circulars may be sent to clients, dealers, sub-dealers, and branches. Official circulars could include guidelines and instructions to employees. Circulars may include a fixed structure which is the address of the issuing agency, reference, date, subject, salutation, body, and finally the signature.

[Model Letter 5-3: Business Proposal (1)]

E & K Cosmetic Co., Ltd.
Jungang-daero, Jung-gu, Busan, Korea
Tel: +82-51-510-1234
Fax: +82-51-510-2000

March 8, 2022

Sun International Co., Ltd.
174, Tambo loom Noi, Samut Sakom, Thailand

Gentlemen:

Your name has been given by the Thailand Chamber of Commerce as one of the reputable importers of Cosmetic Products in your city. And we are writing to you with a keen desire to open an account with you.

We have been established here for over 20 years as exporters of Cosmetic goods. Our products are highly reputed by the importers of China, Makao and Vietnam, etc. We especially introduce about wet sheets for sweaty skin. When you will be a sweaty, if you clean skin for it, your skin will be softly.

In order to diversify our existing market, we are interested in supplying our quality products to you on favorable terms.

We generally do our business on an Irrevocable Letter of Credit, under which we draw a draft at 30 d/s. As to our credit standing, we refer you to the KEB Hana Bank, Seoul.

We look forward to your early reply and favorable reply.

Very truly yours,
E & K Cosmetic Co., Ltd.
Eunhye Bae
Eun-hye BAE
General Manager

[Model Letter 5-4: Business Proposal (2)]

Herbalife Co., Ltd

350 5th Ave, New York, NY 10001

U.S.A.

Dear Sirs,

We are writing this letter because we would like to have a business with you. Your name has been recommended to us by the New York Chamber of Commerce as a large and reliable importer of healthy food in U.S.A.

Our company which was established in 1993 is one of the most reliable and much loved companies selling healthy food in Korea. We hope to expand our business to your country with your company. We are looking forward to exporting our product with high quality but reasonable price.

As to our credit standing, we refer you to the Korea Exchange Bank, Seoul, Korea. Your early reply would be highly appreciated.

Yours very truly,

JM food Co., Ltd

Jeong min Lee

Jeong min Lee

President

[Model Letter 5-5: Reply to Business Proposal (1)]

Sun International Co., Ltd.

174, Tambo loom Noi, Samut Sakom, Thailand

Tel: +66-2-123-4567

Fax: +66-2-123-4568

March 12, 2022

E & K Cosmetic Co., Ltd.
Jungang-daero, Jung-gu, Busan, Korea

Gentlemen:

We thank you very much for your circular letter of March 8 and are willing to enter into business with you.

We have no objection to accepting your proposal so long as your goods prove suitable for our market in price and quality. Please let us have your complete illustrated catalog, samples and price-list.

As to payment, we are agreeable to your terms. If your prices are competitive, we may place a large order with you.

Your best attention to this matter will be much appreciated.

Yours very truly,
Sun International Co., Ltd

Suriyon TUCHINDA

Suriyon TUCHINDA
Vice President

[Model Letter 5-6: Reply to Business Proposal (2)]

JM food Co., Ltd

485 Jang-jcon 3 dong,

Busan, Korea

Jeong min Lee

President

Dear Ms. Lee,

We thank you very much for your circular letter of July 12, 2022. Currently we are considering the possibility of having business with you in case your terms and conditions are proper to us.

Please send us your complete samples and catalogue of healthy food you are handling. Also, we hope to have your price as detailed as possible.

If your price is reasonable and goods are suitable for our market, we will decide to place a large order with you. We look forward to hearing from you soon. Thanks.

Very truly yours,

Herbalife Co., Ltd

Michael J. Simpsons

Michael J. Simpsons

Vice President

3. Credit Inquiry

Global business transactions sometimes face additional difficulties due to differences in language, customs, culture and law, and therefore it is often troublesome to determine whether a potential trade partner will be faithful in honouring the agreement. Realising only too late the fact that a selected trade partner is immoral can often cost the trader unredeemable amounts of time and money to recover from the difficult situation. One of the methods to determine whether the deal will go through as planned is to operate a credit inquiry.

A credit inquiry is usually made focusing on three factors, namely the potential partner's character, capital and capacity, as follows.

i) Character: The first aspect to review is the potential partner's character, the most difficult part of making an assessment of the partner's credit. If a firm fails to properly determine the partner's character, it can face detrimental results. Character refers to the sense of morality, faithfulness, reputation, and overall attitude of an individual or person representing the partnering firm. An exporter is recommended to review the partner's character from the viewpoint of whether this is a real person with whom you could maintain a long-term and serious business relationship.

ii) Capital: The second aspect to review is the potential partner's capital ability, which verifies whether or not the trader has enough funds to make the contracted payments. The importer does not have to be rich himself, but his company needs to have the ability to make payments thorough capital on-hand, projected cash flows or borrowed money. If the importer has a poor credit rating, that is a sign that he has defaulted on payments before, and should raise a red flag.

iii) Capacity: The third aspect to review is the potential partner's capacity to activate the trade. This is a measure of the importer's ability to successfully sell an exporter's products. It is done by analysing the company's history, annual sales, the type of corporation(private or publically traded), experience, marketing rights and abilities, and balance sheet. It is important to make sure that the importer has successfully been growing and developing, or is equipped with sufficient capacity, as indicated by factual evidence. Trading with a company that has filed for liquidation, for example, would not be very advantageous to anyone's business.

In obtaining this information, the importer himself might be the worst source. To ensure getting reliable information, an exporter needs to research the importer, enquire to his/her related banks, business partners, and other references that can give insight into the company's credibility or credit. Sometimes mercantile or credit agencies such as Dun & Bradstreet Information Service(http://www.dnb.com/) or Tokyo Mercantile Agency can be used. If the potential importer is a publically traded company, it will be subject to stricter transparency rules and it will be easier to find financial details.

Credit inquiries can be obtained through banks by using the method of a bank reference or a trade-related organisation, which is called a trade reference. As these organisations only provide actual credit standing, the other factors, including capacity and character, need to be measured separately.

[Model Letter 5-7: Credit Inquiry - To a Bank Reference (1)]

E & K Cosmetic Co., Ltd.
Jungang-daero, Jung-gu, Busan, Korea

Tel: +82-51-510-1234
Fax: +82-51-510-2000

March 14, 2022

Bangkok Bank
333 Silom Road Bangkok, Thailand

Gentlemen:

We would like to start conducting business with SUN International Co., Ltd. 333 Silom Road Bangkok, Thailand. Therefore, we should be much obliged if you would give us such information as you may have or can secure for us regarding their financial standing and reliability.

If possible, your candid opinion on their financial responsibility, their mode of doing business and their general reputation they enjoy your community.

Please charge to our account any expenses connected with this inquiry.

Your prompt attention will be much appreciated, and we assure you that any information which you may provide us will be kept in strict confidence.

Very truly yours,
E & K Cosmetic Co., Ltd.
Eunhye Bae
Eun-hye BAE
General Manager

[Model Letter 5-8: Credit Inquiry (2)]

The Korea Exchange Bank

Seoul, Korea
Dear Sirs:

We have been referred to your bank by JM food Co., Ltd, Busan in their recent proposal to enter into business relations with us.

We shall be very glad if you provide us information about their financial standing, business status and reputation in the market.

Your prompt attention will be higly appreciated and we assure you that your information will be kept in strict confidence.

Very truly yours,
Herbalife Co., Ltd
Michael J. Simpsons
Michael J. Simpsons
Vice President

[Model Letter 5-9: Reply to Credit Inquiry (1)]

Bangkok Bank
333 Silom Road Bangkok Thailand

Tel: +66-1-5746-1111
Fax: +66-1-3755-6729

March 19, 2022

E & K Cosmetic Co., Ltd.
Jungang-daero, Jung-gu, Busan, Korea

Gentlemen:

In reply to your inquiry dated March 14, we are glad to inform you that the firm you inquired about is a highly respectable and well-founded organization, enjoying a first class reputation.

We have done good business with this company for more than ten years, and accept them as the most valuable of our clients.

You will understand, of course, that this information is supplied for your files only and without any responsibility on our part.

Very truly yours,
Bangkok Bank
Thongchai ANANTHOTHAI
Thongchai ANANTHOTHAI
Assistant Manager

[Model Letter 5-10: Reply to Credit Inquiry (2)]

Herbalife Co., Ltd

350 5th Ave, New York, NY 10001, U.S.A.

Dear Sirs,

We are pleased to inform you that the firm referred to in your letter of July 13, 2022.

The company is well-known, respectable and highly reputable company since it was established in 1993 with an authorized capital of US $1,500,000 fully paid-up. Our business relations with them for 30 years have been highly satisfactory. Therefore, we have plenty of confidence in recommending them.

We hope this information will be helpful to you. Also, you will understand, of course, that this information is supplied for your files only without any responsibility on us.

Yours very truly,
The Korea Exchange Bank
Ji Yoon Jeong
Ji Yoon Jeong
Assistant Manager

4. Letter of Trade Inquiry

Letter of Inquiry(LOI) is also known as a business letter of interest. This is one way of letting the concerned individual know that you are interested in having him or her as a business partner. The LOI should show knowledge and professionalism. There are various reasons for writing a letter of inquiry/interest. It can be used when submitting a query or letting a potential employer know about your intention to apply for whatever position in the company. A LOI can be used for business in such a way that it can help you in communicating with your prospective business partner.

• **Format of a Letter of Inquiry(LOI):** A letter of inquiry asks someone for specific information. In some cases, such as a request for promotional material, the recipient will have a clear interest in responding to your letter. In other cases, such as a request for specific information on a product, the recipient may or may not be as motivated to respond quickly. Consequently, always make the tone of the letter friendly and make it easy for the recipient to identify and provide the information you need. Follow the format below in writing a LOI.

① In the first paragraph, identify yourself and, if appropriate, your position, and your institution or firm.

② In the second paragraph, briefly explain why you are writing and how you will use the requested information. Offer to keep the response confidential if such an offer seems reasonable.

③ List the specific information you need. You can phrase your requests as questions or as a list of specific items of information. In either case, make each item clear and concise.

④ Conclude your letter by offering your reader some incentive for responding.

The following letter of inquiry was written by a computer programmer requesting specific information about an upcoming release of a software product.

[Model Letter 5-11: Trade Inquiry (1)]

Sun International Co., Ltd. Tel: +66-2-123-4567
174, Tambo loom Noi, Samut Sakom, Thailand Fax: +66-2-123-4568

March 20, 2022

E & K Cosmetic Co., Ltd.
Jungang-daero, Jung-gu, Busan, Korea

Gentlemen:

Your name and address have been given to us by the Thailand Chamber of Commerce. Your company is a leading firm specializing in cosmetic goods, we wish to make a purchase of wet sheets for sweaty skin from you.

We should be grateful to you if you would quote us for the supply of the items, giving your lowest possible CIF Bangkok prices. And we would also like to have three samples by air mail.

If your goods are satisfactory in quality and delivery, we expect to place regular orders for fairly large numbers.

We hope your prompt attention to this matter and your early reply.

Yours very truly,
Sun International Co., Ltd.
Suriyon TUCHINDA
Suriyon TUCHINDA
Vice President

[Model Letter 5-12: Trade Inquiry (2)]

JM food Co., Ltd

485 Jang-jeon 3 dong, Busan, Korea
Jeong min Lee
President

Dear Ms. Lee:

We have heard from the Korea Exchange Bank in Seoul that your company is reliable and reputable. Therefore, we are giving consideration to a business with your company.

We will be thankful if you let us know your lowest CIF New York prices with earliest delivery schedule. We would also like to have three samples of three good sellers and catalog by air mail from you.

If your goods are satisfactory in quality and delivery and if your price is competitive to us, we will place a large order. We look forward to your early reply. Thanks.

Truly yours,

Herbalife Co., Ltd
Michael J. Simpsons
Michael J. Simpsons
Vice President

[Model Letter 5-13: Reply to Inquiry (1)]

E & K Cosmetic Co., Ltd. Tel: +82-51-510-1234
Jungang-daero, Jung-gu, Busan, Korea Fax: +82-51-510-2000

March 24, 2022

Sun International Co., Ltd.
174, Tambo loom Noi, Samut Sakom, Thailand

Gentlemen:

We thank you for your inquiry of March 20 and are glad to note that you are interested in our wet sheets for sweaty skin. According to your request, we have already dispatched the samples by express delivery

We are separately sending you our offer sheet giving CIF Bangkok prices together with an illustrated catalog for your reference.

If there should be any further information you would like to have, please feel free to let us know.

Very truly yours,
E & K Cosmetic Co., Ltd.
Eunhye Bae
Eun-hye BAE
General Manager

[Model Letter 5-14: Reply to Inquiry (2)]

Herbalife Co., Ltd

350 5th Ave, New York, NY 10001, U.S.A.
Michael J. Simpsons
Vice President

Dear Mr. Simpsons:

Thank you for inquiry dated July 14, 2022 about our three best sellers and catalog.

According to your request, we have already dispatched them by air mail.

From the enclosed catalog including price list, you will notice that our price is reasonable. Our suggestion is that if you order three models which I sent you as samples, we can make them available to you at $20,000 CIF New York.

We look forward to hearing from you soon.

Yours very truly,
JM food Co., Ltd
Jeong min Lee
Jeong min Lee
President

Key Expressions & Technical Terms

✔ **Circular Letter**: A written document that is addressed for circulation to a group of people. It is usually formal and official. It may be for a closed group or general distribution. It may be an effective substitute for a personal visit.

✔ **Credit Inquiry**: Inquiry by a business or person into an entity's credit history. Credit inquiries are used to verify a party's ability to repay some type of loan or monthly payment. Each time a credit inquiry is made, points are deducted from the borrower's credit score. Most inquiries would show up on a credit report provided by one of the three major credit bureaus.

✔ **Letter of Inquiry**: Letter of Inquiry(LOI) is also known as a business letter of interest. This is one way of letting the concerned individual know that you are interested in having him or her as a business partner.

✔ **Overseas Marketing Research(OMR)**: Marketing research related to international or global market is called as overseas marketing research. It refers to collecting data, analyzing data and interpreting data related to foreign markets especially by the exporter.

Check-up Questions 05

Q1 Translate the sentence below into Korean.

At the Information Phase, overseas market research and relevant information for potential business transactions and trading partners, such as credit inquiry, can be acknowledged. Business partners inform themselves about alternative partners for a transaction and their bids, prices, trade terms and further conditions.

➡

Q2 Which one INCORRECTLY describes one of the 4P's of the Marketing Mix for a Target Market?

① Product: Functionality, Brand, Packaging, Services
② Price: List price, Discounts, Bundling, Credit Terms
③ Place: Channel, Inventory, Logistics, Distribution
④ Promotion: Product-use, Publicity, Geography, After-sales Services

Q3 What is NOT considered the basic concept of the business environment?

① Intermediaries
② Suppliers
③ Customers
④ Competitors

Q4 Put the instructions for the format in writing a Letter of Inquiry(LOI) in the correct order.

① Conclude your letter by offering your reader some incentive for responding.

② Identify yourself and, if appropriate, your position, and your institution or firm.

③ List the specific information you need. You can phrase your requests as questions or as a list of specific items of information.

④ Briefly explain why you are writing and how you will use the requested information. Offer to keep the response confidential if such an offer seems reasonable.

➥

Q5 Write the following sentence in English.

당사는 모든 종류의 방송 통신용 음향기기 BCSF-2020/3030 제품을 다량으로 거래하고 있으며, 귀사의 판매조건과 가격이 적당하다면 대량 주문을 하고 싶습니다. 팩스(+82-51-3665-0043)로 조속한 회신을 기다리겠습니다.

[Useful expressions]

- all kinds of products: 모든 종류의 제품
- Broadcasting Communication Sound Facilities: 방송 통신용 음향기기
- on a large scale: 다량으로 거래하는
- favourable terms and conditions: 유리한 조건으로
- prices are reasonable(attractive/favourable): 가격이 적당하다
- sufficient(enough) orders: 충분한 주문
- early(prompt) reply: 조속한 회신
- look forward to V~ing: 기다리다

➥

Q6 Write the following sentence in English.

한국무역협회(KITA)로부터 귀사가 최첨단 가전제품 수출업체라는 것을 알았습니다. 당사는 로봇청소기 RC-1100/RV-1700에 특히 관심이 있사오니, 귀 상품에 관한 보다 자세한 가격표와 도해도, 그리고 카탈로그를 보내주시기를 바랍니다.

➡

Q7 What is NOT one of the main factors for a credit inquiry?

① Character
② Capital
③ Capacity
④ Confidentiality

Q8 Write the following sentence in English.

L&P사는 당사의 각종 자동차제품에 대한 한국 지역 독점판매 대리점으로 지명해 달라는 요구를 팩스로 요청하였고 귀 은행을 신용조회처로 제공하였습니다. 동봉된 봉투로 회신하여 주시면 감사하겠습니다.

[Useful expressions]

- all kinds of auto products: 각종 자동차제품
- exclusive agent: 독점판매 대리점
- to appoint(nominate/designate): 지명하다
- as a reference: 조회처(참조처)로
- provide(supply/furnish/send): 제공하다
- in the enclosed envelope: 동봉된 봉투로

➡

Q9 Write the following sentence in English.

ANGEL사의 영업상태와 평판에 관한 3월 20일자 귀사의 신용조회에 관하여, 동사의 신용도에 대한 우리의 의견은 만족스럽지 않다는 점을 알려드립니다. 이 정보는 사견이며, 그에 관해서 당사는 하등의 책임이 없음을 양지하시기 바랍니다.

[Useful expressions]

- business standing and reputation: 영업상태와 명성
- with regard to your credit inquiry: 신용조회에 관하여
- unfavourable: 불만족스러운
- our personal opinion: 사견이며
- take no responsibility: 하등의 책임이 없다
- please remember (note): 명심하십시오

➡

6
CHAPTER

Global Business English

Agreement Phase

Chapter

6 Agreement Phase

Key Sentences

During the Agreement Phase, negotiations between a supplier and a customer will be held via offer and acceptance, and consideration, and intention to enter into legal relations. At best, it will end in a contract, which determines the rights and duties of the participating parties involved.

Objectives

After studying this lesson, you will be able to:

- understand procedures of business negotiation
- identify the formation of international sale contract

6-1 Establishing Agreement

계약단계에서는 공급자와 고객 간의 협상이 청약과 승낙, 약인, 법적 관계 체결 의사를 통해 이루어진다. 일반적으로 무역계약은 사적 자치의 원칙(The principle of party's autonomy)에 의거하여 당사자 간의 의사의 합치, 즉 합의에 의하여 성립하는데, 의사의 합치는 당사자 일방의 청약(Offer)과 상대방의 승낙(Acceptance)에 의하여 이루어진다.

1. Business Negotiation

Business negotiation is an important part of conducting a global business transaction (GBT) or international trade. It is *the dealings between supplier and customer in*

order to reach agreement on the price, quantity, payment and other terms and conditions of a sale. Obviously, the conclusion of the sales contract results from the business negotiation satisfying both sides.

Global business negotiations are carried out either ***in writing or verbally***. In the latter case, traders talk about the terms and conditions of a transaction with each other in person or by telephone. A foreign businessman may call on the domestic trader upon invitation, or the exporter will make a visit to an overseas importer on his/her own account. Business negotiations are also held at international fairs where businessmen all over the world can negotiate with one another over export and import trade. Through verbal negotiations trading transactions between Korean and foreign businessmen are concluded in large amounts at a number of international trade fairs such as the Seoul International Trade Fair(SITRA).

To reach an agreement of the various terms mentioned above, the global business negotiation ***generally needs to go through five steps: inquiry, offer, counter-offer, acceptance and conclusion of a contract***. Of course, it is not necessary to have all the five steps completed for every transaction. Sometimes, only an offer and acceptance will do. It is stipulated in the laws of some countries that only offer and acceptance are the two required factors, failure to do these will not make a contract. Further details required for establishing an agreement will be discussed below.

[Figure 6-1] Basic Flow of Establishing Agreement for the Sale of Goods Contract between A and B

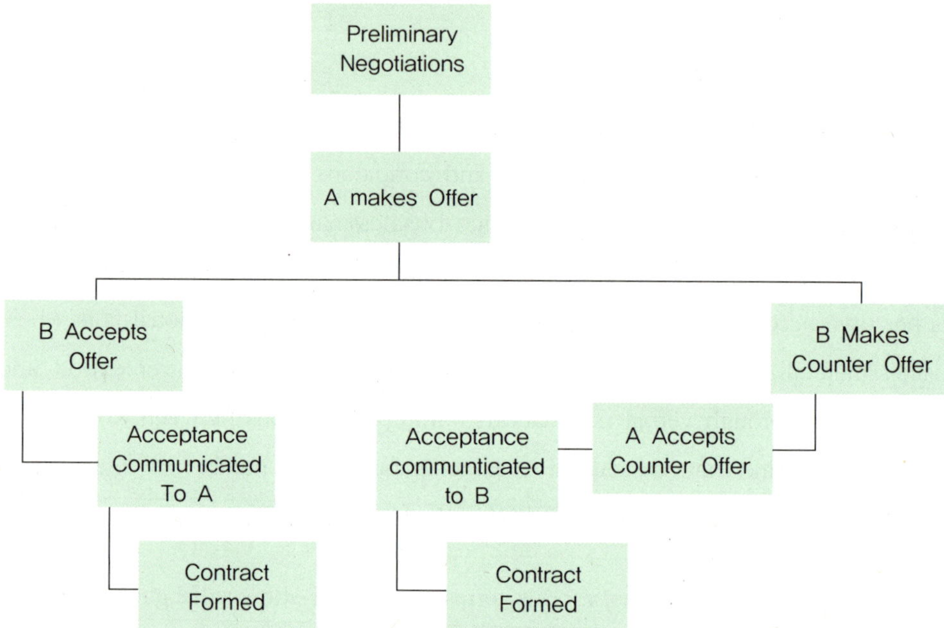

6-2 Formation of International Sales Contract

In the global business transactions(GBT), after business negotiations and having reached an agreement, the two parties of a transaction sign a written contract which shall function as the basis for the performance of rights and obligations by the two parties. Once the sales contract is effectively concluded according to the law, the parties concerned should perform the contract strictly according to the time, quality and quantity as stipulated in the contract. The forming of a contract includes negotiation, conclusion and signing of a contract.

Generally speaking, *a business negotiation involves four steps: offer, counter-offer and acceptance*, among which, offer and acceptance are two indispensable steps for reaching *an agreement and concluding a contract*.

[Figure 6-2] Main Stages of Formation of International Sales Contract

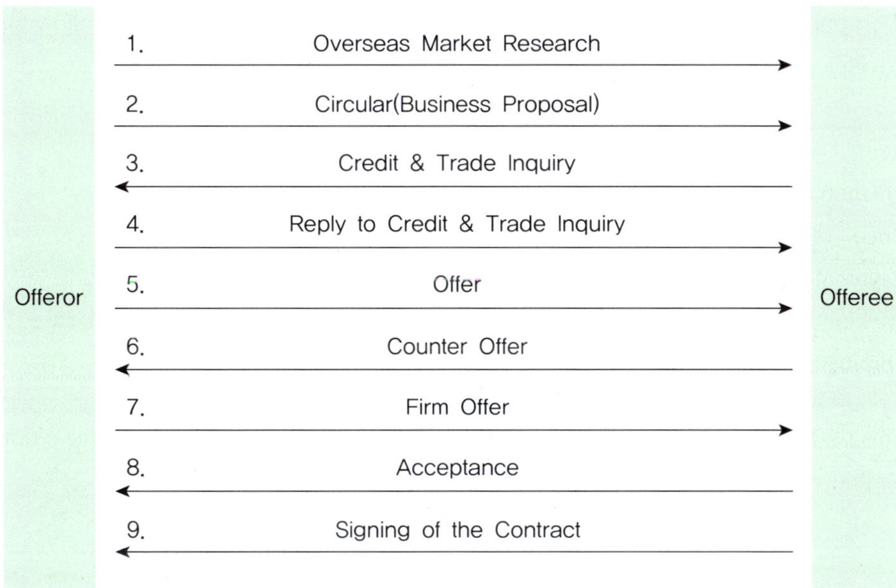

1. Offer

An offer is a proposal addressed to specific persons, i.e. normally from an offeror to an offeree, indicating an intention by the offeror or to be bound to the sale or purchase of particular goods for a price. According to CISG 1980, a proposal for concluding a contract addressed to one or more specific persons constitutes an offer if it is sufficiently definite and indicates the intention of the offer or to be bound in the case of acceptance. A proposal is sufficiently definite if it indicates the goods and expressly or implicitly fixes or makes provisions for determining the quantity.

[Model Letter 6-1: Offer - Firm Offer (1)]

Gentlemen:

We appreciate your inquiry dated October 10. We are glad to E-mail the following firm offer subject to your reply reaching us by October 22.

Item: Dynamic RAM
Quantity: Four Hundred(400) dozen
Price: US$4.50 per dozen C.I.F. New York
Payment: Draft at 30 d/s under an Irrevocable L/C
Packing: 1 dozen each packed in a carton and 100 dozen in a wooden case
Shipment: During November, 2022 by aircraft

This is the best offer we can make at present and we hope to receive your favorable reply soon.

Yours truly,
Min-su Kim
Min-su Kim
Export Manager
KS INTERNATIONAL CO., LTD.

[Model Letter 6–2: Offer – Firm Offer (2)]

E & K Cosmetic Co., Ltd. Tel: +82-51-510-1234
Jungang-daero, Jung-gu, Busan, Korea Fax: +82-51-510-2000

March 30, 2022

Sun International Co., Ltd.
174, Tambo loom Noi, Samut Sakom, Thailand

Gentlemen:

We appreciate your inquiry dated March 20. We are glad to E-mail the following firm offer subject to your reply reaching us by April 15.

Item: Wet sheets for sweaty skin
Quantity: 5,000 pieces
Price: US$7.50 per pc CIF Bangkok
Payment: Draft at sight under an Irrevocable L/C
Packing: 50 pieces each packed in a carton and 500 pieces in a wooden case.
Shipment: During June, 2022

This is the best offer we can make at present and we hope to receive your favorable reply soon.

Very truly yours,
E & K Cosmetic Co., Ltd.
Eunhye Bae
Eun-hye BAE
General Manager

[Model Letter 6-3: Offer - Firm Offer (3)]

Herbalife Co., Ltd

350 5th Ave, New York, NY 10001, U.S.A.
Michael J. Simpsons
Vice President

Dear Mr. Simpsons:

We take great pleasure in offering you the following goods.

Item: Healthy food
Quality: Subject to our samples of No. 1, 2 and 3
Quantity: 100 pieces each(total: 300 pieces)
Price: US $ 70 per piece(total: $ 21,000), CIF New York
Shipment: Within two one month after date of contract

This is the best offer we can make at present and we hope that this offer will meet your acceptance. We are looking forward to your favourable reply soon.

Yours very truly,
JM food Co., Ltd
Jeong min Lee
Jeong min Lee
President

2. Counter Offer

When the buyer finds that the terms and conditions in the offer are acceptable, he/she will probably place an order promptly. However, if the offeree deems the price is on the high side, or does not agree with some of the terms and conditions, he/she may decline the offer, or most probably, make a counter-offer. A reply to an offer which purports to be an acceptance but contains additions, limitations or other modifications is a rejection of the offer and constitutes a counter-offer. Additional or different terms, put forward by the offeree, relating to the price, payment, quality and quantity of the goods, place and time of delivery etc. are considered to alter the terms of offer materially. This means the offeree declined the terms of the offer.

Therefore, a counter-offer is a new offer while at the same time, the original offer lapses. If later, the offeree wants to accept the original offer, because of some favourable changes in the international market prices or in the exchange rate of foreign currencies, the offeror is entitled to decide whether he/she will accept this or not, even if it is within the time of validity of the original offer.

On receiving the counter-offer, the offeror may weigh the advantages and disadvantages and decide to accept or decline it according to the specific situation. He/she may also make a re-offer to put forward some new terms or conditions. This is called anti-counter-offer. Like an offer, a counter-offer is either with engagement or without engagement. A counter-offer in the same way is a firm offer.

[Model Letter 6-4: Counter Offer (1)]

Sun International Co., Ltd. Tel: +66-2-123-4567
171, Tambo Toom Noi, Samut Sakom, Thailand Fax: +66-2-123-4568

April 3, 2022

E & K Cosmetic Co., Ltd.
Jungang-daero, Jung-gu, Busan, Korea

Gentlemen:

Thank you for your E-mail offer of March 30 for 5,000 pieces. Wet sheets for sweaty skin at US$7.50 per piece CIF Bangkok.

Your prices, however, are not competitive and, therefore, we are unable to place an order with you at this time, even though we are favorably impressed with your samples.

Your rival firms are making efforts to get our business by offering much lower prices. But it is our intention to entrust you with the bulk of business, and we have made you a counter offer at US$5.50 per price.

We hope you will take advantage of this chance so that you will benefit from the expanding market.

We look forward to prompt your reply with great interest.

Yours very truly,
Sun International Co., Ltd.
Suriyon TUCHINDA
Suriyon TUCHINDA
Vice President

Encl. Purchase Note

[Model Letter 6-5: Counter Offer (2)]

JM food Co., Ltd
485 Jang-jeon 3 dong,
Busan, Korea
Jeong min Lee
President

Dear Ms. Lee:

We appreciate your recent offer. Your prices, however, are not satisfactory to us. Therefore we are unable to place an order with you at present, even though we are highly impressed with your samples.

We would like to place our order with you because we value the quality of your product. If you can come down to this price level at US $ 20,000 in total, we definitely will make an order with you.

We hope you will take this chance so that you will benefit from the expanding market in America. We look forward to your favourable reply. Thanks.

Truly yours,
Herbalife Co., Ltd
Michael J. Simpsons
Michael J. Simpsons
Vice President

3. Acceptance

In the GBT, the acceptance or a confirmation is the assent to the terms of an offer, required before a contract can be valid. It is indispensable for the conclusion of a business and the signing of a contract indicating that the buyer and the seller have come to an agreement on the sale, it is binding on both parties. An acceptance must meet the following requirements.

① The acceptance must be made *by the offeree*

② The ***contents*** of an acceptance ***must conform*** to that of an *offer*

③ The acceptance must reach the offeror ***within the time of validity of the offer***

④ The acceptance must be in ***oral or written form***

⑤ The acceptance can contain ***NO additions, modifications, or limitations*** to the *offer*

[Model Letter 6-6: Acceptance (1)]

E & K Cosmetic Co., Ltd.
Jungang-daero, Jung-gu, Busan, Korea

Tel: +82-51-510-1234
Fax: +82-51-510-2000

April 10, 2022

Sun International Co., Ltd.
174, Tambo loom Noi, Samut Sakom, Thailand

Gentlemen:

We are glad to accept your counter offer of April 3 in order to realize the first transaction with you.

To confirm this transaction, we are attaching with our revised Offer Sheet No.12. This confirmation is made subject to our Sales Note.

Please note that your limit price barely covers the cost of production, and, therefore, we shall be unable to maintain our quality without any increase in price for your future orders.

We assure you that we will make every effort to meet your satisfaction.

Yours very truly,
E & K Cosmetic Co., Ltd.
Eunhye Bae
Eun-hye BAE
General Manager

Encl. 1 Offer Sheet

[Model Letter 6-7: Acceptance (2)]

JM food Co., Ltd
485 Jang-jeon 3 dong,
Busan, Korea
Jeong min Lee
President

Dear Ms. Lee:

We are glad that you accepted our counter offer with our request for discount at US$20,000 in total.

To confirm this transaction, we are attaching here with our sales note.

In order to cover the amount of this purchase, we have arranged with our bankers for an irrevocable letter of credit to be issued in your favor.

We highly appreciate that your price is reasonable. Since this transaction is very important to us, we would like you to give your best attention to satisfy us in every respect.

Truly yours,
Herbalife Co., Ltd
Michael J. Simpsons
Michael J. Simpsons
Vice President

[Model Letter 6-8: Rejection to Offer]

Dear Sirs,

We are very grateful to you for your offer dated 15th October for 10,000 boxes of paper fasteners.

To our regret, we are unable to accept your offer at the price requested: £15 per 1,000 lbs. You will find on referring to our previous correspondence (August 23rd last) that we quoted you our lowest price for this quantity — £17 per 1,000 lbs.

Since then, prices have risen here, and our profit margin does not warrant any concession by way of quantity reduction or discount.

We should, of course, be glad to accept your offer if you would confirm at £17, per 1,000 lbs, settlement at 30 days after sight.

Yours faithfully,

[Model Letter 6-9: Order]

Gentlemen:

We are very pleased to enclose our Order No. 210 for 150 sets of your Pocket-sized Sense Electronic Calculator Model 8756 according to our fax on May 15.

Since the goods are urgently required, we would appreciate your shipping them as soon as possible and your paying close attention to secure packing.

We have instructed our bankers, The Kookmin Bank, Seoul, to open an irrevocable credit in your favor, and we trust it will reach you soon.

Your prompt attention to this order will be much appreciated.

Very truly yours,

[Model Letter 6-10: Acceptance of Order]

Dir Sirs,

Thank you very much for your order on June 25 for 30,000 yds. of white shirting. We are pleased to confirm our acceptance as shown in the enclosed Sales Note, together with the copy of our cable dispatched today.

We have arranged for immediate shipment as requested. Please open your L/C by telegram by the end of June upon accepting our requirement by cable.

The first available ship is scheduled for departure on the July 15th. We are confident of handling your order with complete satisfaction, providing your L/C reaches us by the end of June.

We hope that this initial business will lead to a pleasant business relationship and further orders in the future.

Yours sincerely,

[Model Letter 6-11: Rejection of an Order]

Dear Sir:

Your shipment of our order No. 123 has yet to reach us as of this date in spite of our repeated requests for urgent dispatch.

Since the goods in this order are all Christmas items, a late delivery will cause us a great loss in our sales. Unless it is delivered by the end of this month at the latest, we have no alternative but to cancel this order.

We anxiously await your immediate response.

Truly yours,

4. Signing of the Contract

In the GBT, the acceptance of an offer or order constitutes a contract. But in accordance with relative Chinese practice and laws, Chinese export and import companies are required to sign a written contract stipulating the rights and responsibilities of the parties concerned with foreign counterparts. After being signed by both parties, a contract will become a formal legal document binding upon both parties. So ***a contract*** is ***an agreement enforceable by law***, by which both the ***buyers and the sellers mutually agree to carry out the trade until it is concluded***. Once the contract has been signed, both parties must ***abide by the contract*** and keep ***good faith***. As a rule, the written contract forms the basis upon which the two parties perform the contract.

[Model Letter 6-12: Sales Confirmation – Purchasing Agreement/Purchasing Order]

TERRIAN TECHNOLOGY INC.

123-45, Yeonyifo-dong, Youngdeunpo-gu, Seoul, Korea (Tel.+82-51-234-5678)

Purchase Order

A. Messrs.	Mr. Kasutonmo Dakuan
KASTOMO Co., Ltd.	Overseas Division
(Address)	

B. Our Reference No.	PO 30231
C. Date	December 31, 2021
D. Out Contact	Mr. Yank-kee Lee

We are please to inform you that we place an order as the following:

E. Item	F. Description	G. Quantity	H. Unit Price(U$)	I. Amount
1. AF 302	Air Filter 2 inch	1,000	3.5	3,500
2. AF 303	Air Filter 3 inch	1,000	4.0	4,000
3. AF 304	Air Filter 4 inch	1,000	4.5	4,500
J. Total Amount				12,000

K. Validity	This PO shall be acknowledged by e-mail within 7 days of issuance.

L. Delivery(Shipment)	Before July 20, 2022
M. Terms of Payment	T/T in advance
N. Insurance	To be effected
O. Incoterms	CIF Incheon
P. Ultimate Destination	Seoul
Q. Carrier Nomination	N/A

R. Other Conditions

① Shipping Notification shall be provided and include estimated date of shipment and expected date of arrival.

② Time is of the essence with respect to delivery. If the Seller is unable for any reason to deliver as specified it shall forthwith give notice to TERRIAN.

③ It the Seller fails to meet the above-mentioned delivery date, the above total amount will be deducted at 1/1000 rate per day as Liquidated Damages.

④ If your document includes modification and/or amendment on the above conditions, it shall be considered as a counter offer rather than an acceptance or order acknowledgement.

⑤ Warranty: Shall be provided for 360 days from the delivery date.

Should you have any further questions, please of not hesitate to contact us.

Signed By(TERRIAN)	Acknowledged By(SELLER)
______________________	______________________
Director, Purchasing Section	Overseas Division
TERRIAN TECHNOLOGY	KASTOMO Co., Ltd.

[Model Letter 6-13: Standard Form Contract – Sales Note]

SALES NOTE

July 25, 2022
No.E15

Messrs. New York Trading, Inc.
125 Broadway, New York
NY 10021, U.S.A.

Dear Sirs,

We, as the seller, confirm having sold you, as the buyer, the following goods on the terms and conditions as in the following pages:

Article:	DVD Player, SDP-777
Quantity:	1,000 sets
Unit Price:	US$282.00
Total Amount:	US$282,000.00
Packing:	2 sets in export carton
Payment:	Draft at sight under an irrevocable L/C

Price Term:	CIF New York
Insurance:	Covering 110% of the invoice value, ICC(B)
Shipment:	Within 3 months after date of this contract
Shipping marks:	NYT
	New York via Panama
	C/N 001-500
	Made in Korea
Documents:	1. Commercial Invoice
	2. Packing List
	3. Full set of clean on board Marine B/L
	4. Marine Cargo Insurance Policy
Remarks:	Your facsimile of July 10 and
	Our letter of July 25

BUYER	SELLER
New York Trading Inc.	Korea Trading Co., Ltd.
____________________	____________________

P.S. Please sign and return the Duplicate to the Seller after confirmation.

GENERAL TERMS AND CONDITIONS

1. BASIS: All business hereafter shall be transacted between the Buyer and Seller on a principal to principal basis.
2. QUANTITY: The quantity set forth on the previous page is subject to variation of five percent (5%) plus or minus at the Seller's option.
3. SHIPMENT: The date of the Bill of Lading shall be accepted as the conclusive date of shipment. A grace period of 20 days shall be allowed for shipment earlier or later than the time agreed by the parties. Partial shipment and transhipment shall be permitted at the option of the Seller unless otherwise stated on the previous page. Each shipment shall be considered as a separate contract. The Seller shall not be responsible for nonshipment or late shipment of the Goods due to failure of the Buyer to provide in time the relative letter of credit or other instructions requested by the Seller or due to failure of the Buyer to comply with the terms and conditions of the Contract in a timely manner.

4. PAYMENT: An irrevocable, without recourse and unrestricted letter of credit at sight in full conformity to this Contract shall be established by the Buyer in favour of the Seller through a bank acceptable to the Seller within 15 days after the conclusion of this Contract and such a letter of credit shall have the validity of at least 15 days after the last day of the month of shipment.
5. INSURANCE: If this Contract is on CIF or CIP basis the insurance shall be effected for one hundred ten percent(110%) of the invoice amount. Any additional premium for insurance coverage over 110% of the invoice amount if so required, shall be borne by the Buyer and shall be added to the invoice amount, for which the letter of credit shall be worded accordingly. If the war risk insurance or other special insurance is deemed necessary by the Buyer or Seller, the Seller shall effect such insurance at the Buyer's expense. Any changes in insurance rates from the rates available at the time of this Contract shall be for the Buyer's account. In this Contract where the Buyer is to effect the insurance, he/she shall give the Seller the necessary information thereof in time for the scheduled shipment.
6. INSPECTION: Unless otherwise instructed by the Buyer, inspection of the Goods performed by a Korean surveyor under the laws and regulations of Korea, manufacturer or Seller, before shipment shall be considered as final. When the Buyer requires a special inspector to perform the inspection of the Goods, the Buyer must inform the Seller of the name of such an inspector at the time of acceptance of the Contract and shall bear any and all costs and expenses to be incurred in connection with such a special inspection. An inspection performed by such a special inspector nominated by the Buyer shall be final.
7. PACKING: Packing, packaging and marking shall be done at the Seller's discretion, unless otherwise specifically provided on the previous page. In the manner customary for the respective merchandise, special arrangements are subject to the buyer's extra charges.
8. CARRIER: In the event that the Buyer nominates a carrier or particular vessel for shipment or nonshipment due to delay or cancellation of or any other causes attributable to such carrier. In such a case, the Buyer shall comply with the Seller's request to amend the letter of credit or any other terms, conditions or procedures necessitated thereby or resulting therefrom.
9. TAXES AND DUTIES: All taxes, duties, costs and charges for the Goods shall be borne and paid by the Buyer.

10. DEFAULTS: In the event of the Buyer neglecting or defaulting his/her parts in this Contract of becoming insolvent, the Seller shall have the option of suspending the performance of or cancelling this Contract, reserving the right to claim against the Buyer for expenses, charges losses and/or market differences caused by such a suspension or cancellation.
11. DISPOSITION OF THE GOODS: In the event of cancellation of this Contract or rejection of the Goods, the Seller shall be entitled to resell of the Goods to third parties, regardless of the trademark, design, patent, copyright, utility model etc., thereon the Buyer shall not raise any objection to such a disposition.
12. INCREASED COST: If the Seller's costs of performance of this Contract increase after the date of this Contract by reason of increased freight rates, taxes or other governmental charges or insurance rates or if any fluctuation in exchange rates increase the Seller's cost or reduce the Seller's earnings, the Buyer shall bear all such increased costs or loss of earnings suffered by the Seller.
13. PATENTS, TRADE MARKS, ETC: The Seller shall not be liable for infringements of patents, designs, trademarks or copyrights involving the Goods. If any dispute arises concerning patents, designs, trademarks or copyrights as the result of the sale of the Goods by the Seller, the Buyer shall, at their own expense, take all such steps as may be necessary to protect themself.
14. WARRANTY: There are no representations or warranties, whether expressed or implied, as to the fitness for a particular purpose of the Goods sold hereunder other than the description on the face of this Contract.
15. WAIVER: Failure of the Seller at any time to require full performance by the Buyer shall not affect the right of the Seller to enforce the same. The waiver by the Seller of any breach of any provision hereof shall not be construed as a waiver of any subsequent breach of any provision or waiver of the provision itself.
16. FORCE MAJEURE: If shipment is prevented or delayed in whole or in part by reason of any prohibition of licenses or any other acts of any government or restriction imposed by any government, war, revolution, riot, strike or other labour disputes, fire, flood, typhoon, peril or accident of the sea, inability to obtain transportation or any other causes beyond the control of the Seller, then the Seller shall not be liable for nonshipment or late shipment of the Goods or for non-performance of this Contract, and the Buyer must accept any shipment made within one month after the termination or removal of any of the aforesaid

causes within prevented the Seller from timely performance of this Contract, or at the Seller's option must accept the termination of all or any part of this Contract in which event the Seller shall have no obligation or liability whatsoever to the Buyer under this Contract.

17. CLAIMS: Any claims by the Buyer regarding the Goods shipped shall be notified by the Buyer to the Seller fully by telex or cable or in writing to the Seller supported by a certificate of an authorised public surveyor within 30 days after the arrival of the Goods at the destination specified in the relative Bill of Lading. A claim made after the said 30 days period shall have no effect and the Seller shall not be obligated to honour it. The Seller shall not under any circumstances be liable for indirect or consequential damages.

18. ARBITRATION: All disputes, controversies, or differences which may arise between the parties, out of or in relation to or in connection with this Contract, or for the breach thereof, shall be finally settled by arbitration in Seoul, Korea in accordance with the rules of the Korean Commercial Arbitration Board under the Laws of Korea. The award rendered by the arbitrators shall be final and binding upon both parties concerned.

19. ENTIRE AGREEMENT: This agreement constitutes the entire agreement between the parties, all prior representations having been merged herein, and may not be modified except in writing signed by a duly authorised representative of both parties.

20. TRADE TERMS AND GOVERNING LAW: The trade terms used herein such as CIF, CIP and FOB shall be in accordance with Incoterms® 2020. In all other respects, this Contract shall be governed by and construed in accordance with the Laws of Korea.

Key Expressions & Technical Terms

✔ **Acceptance**: An express act or implication by conduct that manifests assent to the terms of an offer in a manner invited or required by the offer so that a binding contract is formed. The exercise of power conferred by an offer by performance of some act. The act of a person to whom something is offered of tendered by another, whereby the offered demonstrates through an act invited by the offer an intention of retaining the subject of the offer.

✔ **Counter-Offer**: Acceptance must be made unqualified agreement to the terms of the offer. A purported acceptance which introduces any new terms is a counter-offer, which has the effect of terminating the original offer. It is a final rejection of the original offer. If a counter-offer is made, the original offeror may accept it, but if he or she rejects it the original offer is no longer available for acceptance. A counter-offer may of course be accepted by the original offeror.

✔ **Cross-Offers**: It refers to the offers intersecting each other's mutual offers between offerer and offeree. And if these two offers are identical in terms, cross in the post, there is no contract.

✔ **Firm Offer/Non-Firm Offer**: A firm offer, also called 'offer with engagement', means an irrevocable offer made by a merchant. It is made when a seller promises to sell goods at a stated price and within a stated period of time known as the validity period. As a general rule, all offers are revocable at any time prior to acceptance, even those offers that purport to be irrevocable on their face.

A non-firm offer, also called 'offer without engagement', can be added some statements by offeror on different occasions, such as "the offer is subject to change/alternation without notice", and so on.

So firm offer is more favorable to the buyer than non-firm offer.

✔ **Purchasing Order**: It is a commercial document and first official offer issued by a buyer to a seller, indicating types, quantities, and agreed prices for products or services. It is used to control the purchasing of products and services from external suppliers. Acceptance of a purchase order by a seller forms a contract between the buyer and seller, and no contract exists until the purchase order is accepted.

✔ **Withdrawal of Offer**: An offer becomes effective only after it reaches the offeree. Thus, offers including offers that promise they are irrevocable can be withdrawn prior to their reaching the offeree.

Check-up Questions 06

Q1 The figure below shows the main stages for the Formation of an International Sales Contract. Fill out the missing stages from one to five in both English and Korean.

➡ ①

②

③

④

⑤

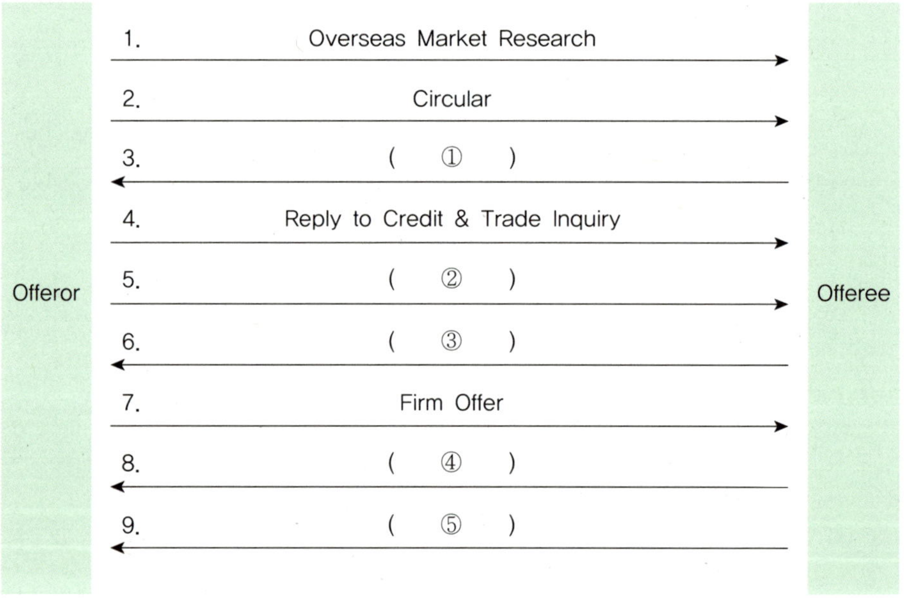

Q2 When suppliers think about clients' reaction to their offers, they often think of the four steps of AIDA. Choose one WRONG description from the following steps.

① 1A=Attracting Attention ② I=Holding Interest

③ D=Creating Demand ④ A=Stimulating Action

Q3 Translate the following paragraph into Korean.

During the Agreement Phase, negotiations between a supplier and a customer will be held via offer and acceptance, and consideration, and intention to enter into legal relationships. At best, it will end in a contract, which determines the rights and duties of the participating parties involved.

➡

Q4 The court will usually look for evidence of three essential elements in any legally-binding contract. Which of the following is NOT correct?

① There must be an agreement usually made by offer and acceptance.
② There must be a bargain by which the obligations assumed by one party are supported by consideration (value) given by the other.
③ The parties must have an intention to create legal relationships between themselves.
④ All contracts must be evidenced in writing.

Q5 Write the following paragraph in English.

귀국으로부터의 주문쇄도로 인해 당사 공장은 당분간 모두 완전히 예약되어 있습니다. 이런 사정을 고려할 때, 당사의 최고품질 의료용기기 SIT-2000/3S의 오퍼가격은 최선의 수준임을 양지하시기 바랍니다.

[Useful expressions]

- due to the rush of orders: 주문쇄도로 인해
- for the time being(for a while): 당분간
- be fully engaged(occupied): 완전히 예약되다

➡

Q6 Write the following paragraph in English.

이번이 귀사와의 첫 정식거래라는 이유로 Super Sensor 6V 모니터 제품 3,000대에 대한 귀사의 주문 NO. 4150을 특별히 수락하기로 결정하였습니다. 당사는 이번 거래가 향후 귀사로부터 대량 주문의 견인차가 되기를 진심으로 바랍니다.

➡

Q7 Write the following paragraph in English.

현재 디지털 S/W 스크린 TV 4001/4002 품목의 재고가 없기 때문에, 지금 당장 주문을 이행할 수 없음을 유감으로 생각합니다. 또한 최근의 주문 폭주로 당사 공장이 매우 바쁘기 때문에 지정 선적기일 내의 인도도 보장할 수 없을 것 같습니다.

[Useful expressions]

- out of stock: 재고품이 없다
- right away(immediately): 지금 당장
- carry out(execute the order): 주문을 이행하다
- the shipping date stipulated: 지정 선적기일
- can not guarantee: 보장할 수 없다

➡

Q8 Which statement does NOT refer to the functions of the contact in written form in the international trade?

① A written contract can take only one form; the sales contract.

② A written contract is evidence of formation of a contract.

③ A written contract is a basis for implementation of a contract.

④ A written contract is sometimes a prerequisite for conclusion of a contract.

Q9 Write the following paragraph in English.

참으로 유감스러운 일이지만, 당사는 알루미늄 AB815제품에 대한 9,000달러 이하의 주문은 모두 거절하고 있습니다. 하지만 소량 주문은 당사의 미국 대리점에서 취급하고 있습니다. L&P사의 제품에 깊은 관심을 가져주셔서 감사합니다.

➡

7 CHAPTER

Global Business English

Implementation Phase: Cargo and Documents Readiness

Chapter

7 Implementation Phase: Cargo and Documents Readiness

Key Sentences

In the Implementation Phase, the exchange of products itself and the according payments, logistics, insurance and customs services take place by delivering goods, providing required documents and paying for the goods as per the performance of the contract and the termination of the contract.

Objectives

After studying this lesson, you will be able to:

- understand the implementation of the contract
- identify contents of cargo and documents readiness
- fill out a commercial invoice

7-1 Buy –Ship – Pay Model

판매자와 구매자 사이에 계약이 성립되면 다음 단계는 계약의 이행이다. 즉, 상품 배송(ship), 보험부보 및 상품 대금결제(pay) 실행이다. 글로벌 비즈니스 트랜잭션(GBT)에서 양 당사자는 계약의 이행에 대한 공동 책임을 진다.

Once a contract is formed between the seller and the buyer, the next step followed is an implementation of the contract; i.e. the execution of the delivery of the goods (SHIP), the coverage of insurance and the payment for the good(PAY). Both parties, in the global business transaction(GBT), will hold joint responsibilities for the performance of the contract.

The seller shall execute its basic obligations of delivering the goods, handing over any documents relating to them and transferring the property of the goods as required by the contract. The seller must deliver goods which are of the quantity, quality and description required by the contract and which are contained or packaged in the manner required by the contract. The seller must deliver goods which are free from any right or claim of the third party, unless the buyer agreed to take the goods subject to that right or claim.

In return, the buyer must arrange financial documents (or instruments) for the payment as required by the contract. The buyer has to choose the financial instruments and the methods of payment, which is pursuant to the terms of payment in the sales contract, and must complete the payment accordingly. The buyer must provide the payment which is free from any right or claim of the third party, unless the seller agreed to accept the payment subject to that right or claim.

7-2 Cargo Readiness

1. Concept of Cargo Readiness

The term cargo readiness is linked to international trade and to a specific date when the shipper (also known as vendor, manufacturer, seller or exporter) has the cargo ready for handover to a transportation provider

This chapter aims to explain exactly what it means to have the cargo ready, and to clear any confusion about which date cargo readiness refers to in the communication between shippers, consignees and freight forwarders. Freight forwarders at times refer to cargo readiness date by the abbreviation CRD.

Cargo readiness can be determined based on specific operational, documentation, and financial-based instructions, events, and other rules, such that the following different cargo readiness types are determined.

Type of Cargo Redainess	Description
Documentation Cargo Readiness(DCR)	Summarizes in documentation terms whether cargo can be loaded or not
Operational Cargo Readiness(OCR)	Summarizes in operational terms whether cargo can be loaded or not
Financial Cargo Readiness(FCR)	Summarizes in financial terms whether cargo can be loaded or not
Aggregated Cargo Readiness(ACR)	Summarizes the documentation, operational, and financial cargo readiness statuses at stage level for a cargo unit

2. The quality must conform to the stipulation of the contract and the requirements of the related laws

(1) Conform to the Contract

When the sale is by description, the goods should comply with the description; when the sale is by sample, the goods should be in accordance with the sample in terms of quality; when the sale is by sample as well as by description, the goods will correspond with both the sample and the description.

(2) Conform to the Requirements of the Related Laws

The requirements by law regarding quality cover two aspects: first the goods are fit for the purpose for which goods of the same description would ordinarily be used, i.e. the goods are merchantable. This is an implied guarantee of quality required by the law. Second, the goods are fit for any particular purpose expressly or impliedly made known to the seller at the time of conclusion of the contract, except where the circumstances show that the buyer did not rely, or that it was unreasonable for him to rely, on the seller's skill and judgement.

3. The quantity must conform to the contract

① The words "about", "approximately" or similar expressions used in connection with the amount of the credit or the quantity or the unit price stated in the credit are to be construed as allowing the quantity or the unit price to which they refer.

② Unless a credit stipulated that the quantity of the goods specified must exceed or be reduced, a tolerance of 5% more or less will be permissible, always provided that the amount of the drawings does not exceed the amount of the credit. This tolerance does not apply when the credit stipulates the quantity in terms of a stated number of packing units or individual items.

7-3 Documents Readiness

According to the sources of document, the most commonly used international trade documents can be classified roughly into five categories as follows.

- Official documents
- Commercial documents
- Financial documents
- Transport documents
- Insurance documents

1. Official Documents

A GBT involves complex flows of goods and services between many countries. Therefore, a set of official documents are used by countries to monitor and control these flows. These usually include.

- Export License
- Import License and foreign exchange authorisation

- Certificate of Origin
- Inspection Certificate
- Consular Invoice
- Customs Invoice

(1) Export License

Export license is also called the export permit, which is the first document an exporter must be concerned with. Such a document is normally required for the export of certain key raw material, equipment, machinery or other restricted goods related to national or international security; or works of arts or antiques that are of national, cultural or historical importance. It may also be required to implement a government policy or decisions, such as to exercise economic sanctions against some countries. This document is taken by many as the lock-up preventing the exporter from pushing his/her goods to the foreign market. Processing the export license always experiences several steps such as application, submission, classification, evaluation, issuance or refusal.

(2) Import License and Foreign Authorisation

Many countries use import licenses and foreign authorisation systems to restrict importers from presenting pro forma invoices to their licensing authorities or to their central banks, or sometimes to both to apply for the license. If the planned importation is legal and meets current requirements, the license will be issued. Therefore, exporters should not ship to importers who need licenses until the licenses are actually in hand. The purpose of such documents is to control the inflow of foreign goods for various purposes such as to protect the domestic industries, or maintain the balance of payments or to implement a political polity, etc.

(3) Certificate of Origin

A certificate of origin is the document which states the country or the place of origin of the goods. It is a form to prove that the merchandise in question did come from wherever it is claimed. The certificate is usually prepared by the shipper, signed in the presence of a notary public, and then certified by a non-governmental commercial organisation acceptable to the country of destination. The main purpose is to obtain preferred import status for the goods and to get financing easily for the export of goods of certain origin. It is usually required by countries that do not use a Customs Invoice or Consular Invoice to set appropriate duties for the import. It contains the nature, quantity, values of goods shipped and their place of manufacture. There is no standard format for a certificate of origin and indeed no specific format is required for most nations. The exporter must at all times be ready to obtain a certificate if requested for any export shipment.

In Korea, this certificate is generally issued by the Korea Chamber of Commerce & Industry(KCCI), or Korea Customs Service.

[Model Letter 7–1: Certificate of Origin]

<table>
<tr><td>1. Exporter (Name, address, country)

GILDONG TRADING CO. LTD
15P. SAMSUNG-DONG, KANGNAM-GU
SEOUL, KOREA</td><td colspan="2">ORIGINAL

CERTIFICATE OF ORIGIN

issued by

THE KOREA CHAMBER OF COMMERCE & INDUSTRY

Seoul, Republic of Korea</td></tr>
<tr><td>2. Consignee (Name, address, country)

TO ORDER OF abc BANK</td><td colspan="2">3. Country of Origin

REPUBLIC OF KOREA</td></tr>
<tr><td>4. Transport details
FORM: BUSAN, KOREA
TO: NEW YORK, USA
BY: SAZLING ON OR ABUT
ARP 25, 2022</td><td colspan="2">5. Remarks

CY 875-024-4 APR 25, 2022</td></tr>
<tr><td colspan="2">6. Marks & numbers; number and kind of packages; description of goods

G.T.
NEW YORK
S/#: 4794FX
GT/FXMR
E/#: 1
Q'TY: 2 DOZ
C/#: 1-400
MADE IN KOREA
///////////////////////////////

LADIES 55PCT RAMIE 45 PCT COTTON
SWEATERS.
CAT 845
(55% RAMIE 45% COTTON 2/17's)
STYLE NO/ 4794FX GT/FXMR
L/C NO. Y 178972
///</td><td>7. Quantity

800 DOZ
//////////////////////////</td></tr>
<tr><td>8. Declaration by the Exporter

(Signature)

(Name)</td><td colspan="2">9. Certification

Authorized Signatory

Certificate No.</td></tr>
</table>

(4) Certificate of Inspection

This document contains many similar kinds of certificates, e.g. certificate of value, certificate of quality, certificate of quantity, certificate of health, and weight memo, etc. The contract may require either the exporter to certify that the quality of the goods meets the contract requirements of an external inspector to make an independent certification. The contract also stipulates who is to carry out the inspection and who is to pay for it. The purpose is to ensure that the goods meet a certain standard. The inspection is done by either governmental authorities such as the Ministry of Food and Drug Safety, National Quarantine Station, or Animal and Plant Quarantine Agency, etc., or other independent certified organisations such as Korea Inspection Co., Ltd., Lloyd's Surveyor, Lloyd's Agent, SGS, GESCO, FESCO, INTECO, and United States Consults Inc., etc.

[Model Letter 7-2: Certificate of Inspection]

견 본

KOREA INSPECTION CO., LTD

50, Namdaemun-Ro 1Ga, Jung-gu Seoul, 100-710 Korea

Tel:(82-2)316-3302/Fax:(82-2)316-3500

INSPECTION CERTIFICATE

(NO.KIC2002-05-2, DATE : 31. MAY. 2002)

* DESCRIPTION OF GOODS : 100% POLYESTER WOVEN FABRIC
58" HI COUNT DTY T/F

	42,800MTS	12,784KG	13,500KG
TOTAL	42,800MTS	12,784KG	13,500KG

AS PER BENE.' P/I NO. HKD2002-05 DATE : 15. MAY. 2002

* DOCUMENTARY CREDIT NUMBER 1200/[illegible]/CD
* L/C ISSUING BANK BANK SEPAH FERDOSI SQ, BR., FERDOSI SQ., P.C. 11319, TEHRAN, IRAN TEL NO. 6709664 FAX NO. 6711725

* CUSTOMS TARIFF NO. 7210/69

* SHIPMENT FROM BUSAN-KOREA TO BANDAR ABBAS PERSIAN GULF BY CLASSIFIED VESSEL IN CONTAINER.
* NAME OF VESSEL APL MALAYSIA 104W

* NOTIFY PARTY PARS KHAZAR INDUSTRIAL CO. THERAN/IRAN CREDIT NUMBER.1200/80504642/CD

* BENEFICIARY HONG KIL DONG CO., LTD 45, NAMDAEMUN-RO 4GA, JUNG-GU SEOUL 100-743 KOREA

* MANUFACTURER HONG KIL DONG CO., LTD
* PACKING CASE IN CONTAINER
* TOLERANCE TOTAL QUANTITY +0/-10PCT

WE HERBY CONFIRM AND VERIFY THAT GOODS ARE PRODUCED IN CONFORMITY WITH STANDARD K.I.C C3314 AS DECLARD BY MANUFACTURER/SUPPLIER.
Sworn before us that the foregoing to be true and correct.

KOREA INSPECTION CO., LTD

KimDaeHan

KIM DAE HAN/ GERNERAL MANAGER

(5) Consular Invoice

A consular invoice is a document certified by the consul of the country which the merchandise is destined and an exporter must purchase from the importing country's commercial Consulate. The invoice is used by customs officials of the country of entry to verify the value, quantity, and nature of the merchandise imported. Most of the consular invoices are in the language of the country from which the goods are shipped. It is the most difficult document of all and must be filled in with extreme care.

(6) Customs Invoice

Customs invoices are required by the importing country in order to clear customs, to compile statistics, to verify country of origin for import duty and tax purposes, to compare the exporting price and domestic price, and to fix the anti-dumping duty. It is issued on a special form prescribed by the customs authorities of the importing country.

2. Commercial Documents

Commercial documents are generally issued by the importer, or some relevant non-governmental business organisations. They aim to ensure smooth transactions and usually include.

- Pro Forma Invoice
- Commercial Invoice
- Quality Certificate
- Weight Certificate

(1) Pro Forma Invoice

Pro forma invoice is an invoice similar to a commercial invoice and it contains the same information as a commercial invoice but is headed Pro Forma. It is provided by an exporter prior to a sale or shipment of merchandise, informing the buyer of the kinds and quantities of goods to be shipped, their value, the specifications as per weight, size and similar characteristics. A pro forma invoice is used as a preliminary invoice together with a quotation; it is used for quotation to the importer who sometimes needs this document to apply for import licenses and foreign exchange. Specifically, an irrevocable letter of credit is required by the exporter, the importer will use it to substantiate the need for a letter of credit to his/her bank, or the importer's country requires that an import license be issued for each import and must approve the pro forma invoice before making foreign exchange available for payment by the importer.

Therefore, a pro forma invoice has no legal status. It is only a means to facilitate the buyer to accomplish the corresponding tasks.

(2) Commercial Invoice

A commercial invoice is one of the most important documents which identifies the seller and the buyer of goods or services, numbers such as the invoice number, date, shipping date, mode of transport, delivery and payment terms, and a complete list and description of the goods or services including prices, discounts and quantities. It is often used by governments to determine the true value of goods for the assessment of customs duties and also to prepare consular documents. Governments often specify its form, content, and numbers of copies, language to be used, and other characteristics to control imports.

Commercial invoices used in international trade serve as a record of the essential details of a transaction. Therefore, great attention should be given to the fact that the commercial invoice must be totally accurate in all respects. If the document received by the importer has mistakes, it may lead to excessive duties or fines and penalties. A commercial invoice must show the following basic information about the transaction.

① *The shipper*: The full and accurate name of the shipper should be used.

② *The description*: Description of the goods in the commercial invoice must be in exact conformity with that spelled out in the letter of credit(L/C) and other documents.

③ *Net and gross weight*: Depending upon the product, duty may often be applied on the weight of the goods, and if the net and the gross weights are not stated, the customs authorities may just take the gross weight as the weight for duty.

④ *The dimension of the shipment*: For handling the goods in transit.

⑤ *The unit price*: The most important information in the invoice; some countries will levy a fine against you if you show a price lower than that agreed upon; and carefully note the "currency" in which the price is listed to make sure that this conforms to that stipulated in the contract.

⑥ *Freight, insurance, package*: Must be in conformity with whatever is designated in the agreement, but also agree with the actual charges which may be reflected in other documents such as the freight on the bill of lading(B/L).

⑦ *Date*: To date the invoice because this could be a determining factor in the date of payment.

⑧ *Signature*: Omission of the currency designated is the most common error on the invoice, and a failure to sign the invoice comes a close second.

[Model Letter 7-3: Commercial Invoice – Example]

COMMERCIAL INVOICE

① Shipper/Seller Hansol Automobile Tire Inc. C.P.O. Box No.7917 Seoul. Korea		⑧ No. & date of invoice HS-070613 June 13, 2022 ⑨ No. & date of L/C IMP20748 March 15, 2022
② For account & risk of Messers. Wilson & Company, Limited 50 Liberty Street New York, N. Y. 10001		⑩ L/C issuing bank CHASE LINCOLN FIRST BANK N.A.
③ Notify party Same as above		⑪ Remarks : Details are as per P/O No.DIC-07-03-10 Dated March 10, 2022 to be issued by Wilson & Company, Limited. Origin : Republic of Korea
④ Port of loading Busan, Korea	⑤ Final destination New York, U.S.A.	⑫ Payment Terms Letter of Credit. At sight
⑥ Carrier m.s. Brown 709E	⑦ Sailing on or about June 15, 2022	⑬ Price Term : CIF Busan, Korea

⑭ Marks & numbers of Pkg	⑮ Description of Goods	⑯ Quantity	⑰ Unit-price	⑱ Amount
"WS" IN TRIANGLE C/NO : 1-2500 USD 171,500.00 ITEM : AUTO TUBE SIZE : Q'TY :	AUTOMOBILE TUBE SIZE VALVE 500R13 TR13	50,000PCS	USD3.43	USD171,500.00

//

P.O.Box :
E-mail :
Telefax No. :
Telephone No. :

⑲ Signed by ____________________
Manager

(3) Quality Certificate

A quality certificate confirms that the quality/specification of a particular consignment of goods is in agreement with the sales contract at the time of shipment. It may be issued by the exporter or a relevant government department as required under the L/C or sales contract terms. It is essential that cargo description in the quality certificate conforms to its terms found in other relevant documents, such as the commercial invoice, L/C, insurance policy.

[Model Letter 7-4: Quality Certificate - Certificate of Conformity]

Certificate No. MGK-25

CERTIFICATE OF CONFORMITY

Name of Manufacturer, Address

NEO VISION CO., LTD.

592-35 Galsan-dong, Icheon-city, Gyeonggi-do, Korea

Name of Product(s)

Soft contact lens, Hard contact lens

It is certified that the Quality System of the above mentioned products has been found to comply with the requirements of the Korea Quality System Regulation(GMP) for Medical Devices.

Originally Certified : February. 26. 2007
Latest issue : February. 26. 2007
Expiry Date : February. 25. 2010

Head of Certification

Bo Won . Lee

KTR

Korea Testing and Research Institute

KTR is The Quality System Auditing Organization
accredited by the Commissioner of KFDA

(4) Weight Certificate

A Weight certificate is usually requested by the importer to confirm that the weight of the goods is in accordance with the sales contract at the time of shipment. It is a supplement to a commercial invoice to show that details of a shipment when specification, quantity, weights or contents of individual units in the shipment vary. Similar to a quality certificate, it may be issued by the exporter or a relevant government department as required under the L/C or sales contract terms. The purpose of a weight certificate is to recognise the goods, to clear the customs and to check the goods.

Key Expressions & Technical Terms

✔ **Certificate of Conformity(CoC)**: Type Approval or Certificate of Conformity is granted to a product that meets a minimum set of regulatory, technical and safety requirements. Generally, type approval is required before a product is allowed to be sold in a particular country, so the requirements for a given product will vary around the world. Processes and certifications known as Type Approval in English are generally called Homologation, or some cognate expression, in other European languages.

✔ **Certificate of Origin**: A certificate of origin(often abbreviated to C/O, COO or CoO) is a document used in international trade. In a printed form or as an electronic document, it is completed by the exporter and certified by an recognized issuing body, attesting that the goods in a particular export shipment have been produced, manufactured or processed in a particular country.

✔ **Commercial Invoice**: A commercial invoice is a document used in foreign trade. It is used as a customs declaration provided by the person or corporation that is exporting an item across international borders. Although there is no standard format, the document must include a few specific pieces of information such as the parties involved in the shipping transaction, the goods being transported, the country of manufacture, and the Harmonized System codes for those goods. A commercial invoice must also include a statement certifying that the invoice is true, and a signature.

✔ **Customs Invoice/Consular Invoice**: Extended form of commercial invoice required by customs(often in a specified format) in which the exporter states the description, quantity and selling price, freight, insurance, and packing costs, terms of delivery and payment, weight and/or volume of the goods for the purpose of determining customs import value at the port of destination.

- ✔ Fair Average Quality(F.A.Q): An import license is a document issued by a national government authorizing the importation of certain goods into its territory. Import licenses are considered to be non-tariff barriers to trade when used as a way to discriminate against another country's goods in order to protect a domestic used to describe food products such as grain, fruit, etc. that are of a good enough quality to be sold.

- ✔ Inspection Certificate: Required usually for import of industrial equipment, meat products, and perishable merchandise, it certifies that the item meets the required specifications and was in good condition and correct quantity when it left the port of departure. Also called inspection certificate or inspection report.

Check-up Questions 07

Q1 Translate the paragraph below into Korean.

In the Implementation Phase, the exchange of products itself and the according payment, logistics, insurance and customs services take place by delivering goods, providing required documents and paying for the goods as per the performance of the contract and the termination of the contract.

➡

Q2 Translate the paragraph below into Korean.

Documentation means an act of furnishing or authentication of all or any of the documents relating to a transaction. Domestic businesses and GBTs both need some documents, but in exporting and importing it is necessary for each shipment to be accompanied by a variety of documents, therefore, it can be said that the major difference between domestic and overseas trade is that there are more documents for every export or import shipment.

➡

Q3 Translate the paragraph below into Korean.

In the global business transaction and contract negotiation, both the buyer and seller must make sure of the commodity intended for the transaction and describe the goods in the sales contract precisely. As far as commodity in trade is concerned, it comprises of the name of the commodity, quality of the commodity, quantity of the commodity, packing of the commodity, making of the commodity and commodity inspection.

➡

Q4 Explain the following words and make a document.

① Certificate of Origin

② Commercial Invoice

③ Quality Certificate

④ Weight Certificate

8

CHAPTER

Global Business English

Implementation Phase: International Transportation

Chapter

8 Implementation Phase: International Transportation

Key Sentences

International transportation is the term we use to describe the delivery of goods from one country of origin to a different country as a destination point. destination point.

Objectives

After studying this lesson, you will be able to:

- understand the types of international transportation
- identify characteristics of international transportation
- fill out a transport document

국제무역 장벽이 낮아짐에 따라 양자간 또는 다자간 무역은 일부 국가 경제의 성장보다 3~4배 빠르게 증가한다. 운송은 경제 자원의 이용 및 개발과 함께 점점 더 중요한 역할을 한다. 수출거래를 수행하고 상품이나 재화를 안전하고 효율적이며 신속하고 경제적으로 운송하기 위해서는 운송에 대한 해박한 지식을 습득하는 것이 사업가에게 도움이 될 것이다. 화물운송은 해상, 철도, 항공, 내륙수로, 소포·우편, 컨테이너 적재, 팔레트 적재 또는 복합 운송을 통해 이루어질 수 있다.

With the lowering of international trade barriers, international bilateral or multilateral trade increases three or four times faster than the growth of some national economies. Transport plays increasingly important roles with the development and exploitation of economic resources. In order to fulfil an export transaction and transport goods or commodities in a safe, efficient, speedy, prompt and economical way, a business person will find it helpful to command a good knowledge of transport.

The way goods move from one city to another hasn't changed much over the years. Transportation of goods may be by sea, rail, air, inland waterway, parcel post, container loading, pallet loading or intermodal transport. What has changed is the size of the shipment and how it is monitored by the software.

These days, we see small-volume custom orders, an increase in e-commerce in logistics, and an increase in frequency of deliveries. There has been a tremendous amount of innovation and that has made transportation much more agile. This chapter describes the different types of transport used in the logistics industry.

8-1 Types of Transportation

1. Sea Transportation

Carriage by Sea or Marine Transportation is the most widely used mode of transportation in international trade as well as the most efficient form in terms of energy. Two thirds of the world total volume and the majority of Korea's imports and exports are transported by sea. The first advantage is the easy passage since about 70% of the earth surface is covered by water. It still has the attraction of being a cheap mode of transport delivering large quantities of goods over long distances. Because of the large capacity of ocean shipping, the unit distribution cost is reduced. Furthermore, ocean transport has good adaptability to cargoes of different size, weight, shape, etc. However, it is slow, vulnerable to bad weather and less punctual if compared with road or air transport. Therefore, before a shipment is made, the exporter has to consider many different factors influencing transport considerations, e.g. cost, safety, speed and convenience.

2. Air Transportation

Air transportation is one of the youngest forms of distribution. It is reported that air cargo represents about 13% of world airline revenue and it increases at the rate of 7-8% each year. Most air cargoes are carried on passenger airlines, about 80% of air cargoes are transported by IATA(International Air Transport Association) members.

Air freight is most desirable for consumer cargoes such as fresh flowers and fruits which will deteriorate easily, fashionable articles that have a short selling life, seasonal goods or merchandise of high value but low volume.

The most outstanding attraction of air freight is quick transit. Quick, reliable transits eliminates the needs for warehouses and reduces the risk of stockpiling, obsolescence, deterioration and capital tied up in warehouse and stock provision. A low risk of damage and pilfering with consequent competitive insurance premiums is another advantage. However, the average aircraft capacity is only 2,000-2,500 kg, so air transport is subject to a high operating cost when compared to its overall capacity. In addition, when airlines or air cargo companies issue an air waybill, it is often a straight waybill, the buyer is named as the consignee on the waybill, so he/she can claim the cargoes from the carrier by simply showing proof of identity. For this reason, air freight must be a risky way to ship goods.

3. Rail Transportation

This mode of logistics transportation is not just sustainable but is also quicker compared to shipping and much affordable compared to air operations.

Railway transportation is no doubt the most reliable way of transport. Compared to marine and road transport, rail is rarely influenced by weather conditions. Transport trains will run in the snow, fog, rain, and other conditions that would otherwise delay shipments brought by other methods. Rail is barely not influenced by weather conditions.

Railway service is more accurate compared to other modes of shipment with fixed schedules running regularly. On top of that, rail transport provides massive carrying capabilities that can increase to fit your requirements.

4. Road Transportation

Road transport means transportation of goods and personnel from one place to the other on roads. The investment required in road transport is very less compared to other modes of transport such as railways and air transport. The cost of construction, operating cost and maintaining roads is cheaper than that of the railways.

If goods are intended to be delivered right away, your best bet would be road shipping transportation. You will find many benefits to this mode of transportation, particularly for organizations depending on fast delivery to keep their customers. Water transport is extremely slow, and it could be a trouble to book a railway transport as well.

5. Intermodal Transportation

Intermodal Transportation refers to the movement of large cargoes in two or more modes of transport in the same steel-based container. It's a typical way of moving goods in modern times. Intermodal transfer may involve truck, rail, ship, and then truck again. Basically, instead of shifting goods from one vehicle to the next in their journey, intermodal transport handles these special standardized containers instead. This process offers many advantages such as lower rates, flexibility, predictable pricing, standardized delivery schedules, improved product safety and faster delivery.

[Figure 8-1] Examples of International Cargo Transportation

Sea Transport

Air Transport

Road Transport

Rail Transport

Inland Waterway Transport

Containerisation

Palletisation

Pipelines

Int'l Multimodal Transport

8-2 Transportation Documents

A single export shipment can involve a lot of different documents to ensure that the goods reach the final consignee. A few commonly used transportation documents are listed below.

- Bill of Lading(B/L)
- Mate's Receipt(M/R)
- Sea Waybill
- Packing List
- Rail Consignment Note
- Road Consignment Note
- Air Waybill
- Combined Transport Documents
- Arrival Notification

1. Bill of Lading(B/L)

A bill of lading, i.e. the most important document for sea transport, is a document issued by a carrier to a shipper, signed by the captain, agent, or owner of a vessel, stating the conditions in which the goods were delivered to (and received by) the ship; and an engagement to deliver goods at the prescribed port of destination to the lawful holder of the B/L. A B/L is, therefore, both a receipt for merchandise and proof of a contract to deliver it as freight. It is a document of title to the goods, enabling the shipper or owner of the goods to endorse title to other parties, sell goods in transit, and present to banks with other documents in seeking payment under documentary credits.

2. Mate's Receipt(M/R)

A mate's receipt(M/R) is a declaration issued by a chief officer(or a mate) of a vessel in the name of the shipping company stating that certain goods have been received on board his/her vessel. It serves the shipping company as a delivery or receipt note for particular consignment. That's why it is also called a shipping note, which is not a title document, but just used as an interim document until the B/L is issued. It gives information about a particular export consignment when offered for shipment. The cargo description in an M/R should conform to that found on the commercial invoice.

3. Sea Waybill

Shipping companies issue sea waybills(SWB) to shippers as a sort of proof or evidence that there is a contract of carriage between the shipper in question and the shipping company. In other words, the SWB is a document that serves as proof that the shipper actually received the goods from the shipper and agreed to carry it to a stated destination. In a sense, the SWB is similar to the B/L, which is the main shipping document.

The SWB is important because it serves as an alternative for a B/L for the purposes of shipping goods and having someone collect the goods on arrival at the destination port. The reason why this document is necessary is because the B/L might take a much longer time to arrive because of situations such as postal delays and other unforeseen circumstances. In this sense, the SWB also serves as an authorization for the goods covered by the document to be released to the consignee named on the document. Such a precaution helps shippers expedite the process of offloading the cargo on arrival at their final destination. Without the waybill, they might be obliged to wait for the arrival of the various B/L for the different cargos, which might delay the offloading process.

One major distinction between an SWB and a B/L is that the B/L can transfer title, but the SWB cannot. This means that the B/L can be used as a form of collateral, unlike the SWB. The reason for this is because the name of the consignee on the SWB is locked and cannot be changed after it has been issued by the owner of the cargo. On the contrary, the owner of the cargo or the person whose name is on the B/L can transfer the title to anyone.

4. Packing List

This document is really an addendum to the commercial invoice when numerous units of the same product are being shipped or when quantities, weights or contents of individual units in a shipment vary. Occasionally, a separate list is prepared for each package showing the weight and measurements and contents, which helps identify the specific item by the importer and facilitate customs clearance. Upon arrival of the goods, customs may carry out a partial examination by checking a certain number of the cases. If the packing list proves to be accurate, the rest of the shipment is assumed to be in order.

5. Rail Consignment Note

A consignment note for rail transport serves as *prima facie* evidence of the contract of carriage between the railway and consignor, by evidencing the receipt of the goods and the date of acceptance for carriage by the carrier. The consignment note will be delivered with the cargo from the departure station to the consignee at the destination station against payment of the amounts by the consignee. Unlike a B/L, it is not a document of title and is not transferable or negotiable. The seller should be responsible for the accuracy of the information in the consignment note. The railway has the right to check if the consignment corresponds with the information in the consignment note.

6. Road Consignment Note

A road consignment note, similar to rail consignment note in form and contents, functions as *prima facie* evidence for the contract of the carriage of goods by road in vehicles, completed by the sender and carrier with the appropriate signatures and/or stamp. Like a rail consignment note, it evidences the place and date of taking over the goods and the place designated for delivery. It is not a negotiable or transferable document or document of title.

7. Air Waybill

The air waybill(AWB) is one of the most important cargo documents prepared and issued by a carrier or its authorised cargo agents. It is the shipping document when the goods are shipped by air. It is proof of acknowledging receipt of the goods from the shipper by the airline, evidence of a contract between the shipper and the airline for moving the goods, a certificate of insurance, a customs declaration, and an instruction sheet guiding the carrier's staff in handling the cargo.

The AWB is an internationally standardised document printed in English or the language of the air carrier. AWB is a straight or non-negotiable form of B/L. Until now, no "to order" or negotiable AWBs are issued by IATA (International Air Transport Association) members. Therefore, the word "non-negotiable" must not be crossed out or tampered with in any way.

8. Combined Transport Document

A Combined Transport Document (or Multimodal Transport Document) proves the contract of carriage of goods by at least two modes of transport, issued by a combined transport operator under a combined transport contract. It is quite similar to "through B/L" and combined transport B/L used for ocean transport, but is broader than them. Through B/L and combined transport B/L are always connected with the sea, and used for any transport combined with the sea, while combined transport documents can be applied to any kind of combined transport. Several carriers are involved in the through B/L, while the combined transport document is issued by only one carrier, that is, the combined transport operator. The combined transport document can be made as either negotiable or non-negotiable.

9. Arrival Notification

An arrival notification is the document furnished to the consignee and shipping broker giving notice to them of the up-coming arrival of freight and availability of freight for pick-up. It also requires the consignee to submit appropriate documents, such as the original B/L, for customs clearance. Thus, the carrier can subsequently dispatch the goods to the consignee.

8-3 Model Letter of Ship – Transportation

[Model Letter 8-1: Shipping Advice (1)]

To whom it may concern:

We are pleased to inform you that today we have shipped your order No. 567 for 250 units of cameras on the M/S Pacific of PK Line leaving Incheon on July 27 as per enclosed copies of the relative shipping documents.

To cover this shipment, we have drawn on your bank a 60 d/s draft for the full invoice amount of U.S. $32,000.00 under L/C No.5678 through the Hana Bank, Seoul. We hope you would honour the draft upon presentation.

We hope that your goods will arrive in good order and that you will find them satisfactory.

Yours faithfully,

[Model Letter 8-2: Shipping Advice (2)]

To whom it may concern:

Shipping Advice

We are pleased to confirm by cable dated August 31 advising you of shipment of our Color Television Sets AB201 against your Order No. 56 by M.V. "Kumgang-ho" that left here on August 30. As advised by the same cable we had to switch to this boat last month due to a sudden cancellation of the scheduled steamer. However, we are happy to tell you that since the "Kumgang-ho" left the port on the same day of shipment as stipulated in the L/C there was no delay in our schedule.

Enclosed are copies of the shipping documents as follows:

No. of copies.
a. Invoice 3
b. Certificate of Origin 1
c. Bill of Lading 1
d. Packing List 1
e. Insurance Policy 1
f. Inspection Certificate 1

We trust that your order will reach you in good condition and ask you to accept our draft upon presentation.

We look forward to your further orders.

Very truly yours,

[Model Letter 8-3: Dispatch by Air]

To whom it may concern:

Dispatch: Order No. 351

We confirm the dispatch of your packages containing Watch Parts by BA Flight No.320 to London this afternoon.

Enclosed is our Invoice No. TYBS1007-25 covering these parts. The cost of insurance and freight, which is payable by you, has been included in the document. We expect your payment in due course.

We shall be pleased to receive further orders from you.

Yours faithfully,

[Model Letter 8-4: Delay in shipment]

Dear Sir:

We are sorry to inform you that an accident in the machines of our maker's factory made it impossible for us to ship the goods on your order No. 423 by 30th December as arranged.

Therefore, we sent you a fax yesterday asking for postponement of shipment till the 8th January. The goods will be sent out by a direct steamer leaving our port on that day.

We are indeed very sorry to have troubled you so much, and assure you that we will be more careful not to repeat such a failure.

Yours faithfully,

[Model Letter 8-5: Bill of Lading(B/L)]

Bill of Lading

① Shipper/Exporter ABC TRADING CO. LTD. 1. PIL-DONG, JUNG-KU, SEOUL, KOREA	⑪ B/L No. : But 1004
② Consignee TO ORDER OF XYZ BANK	
③ Notify Party ABC IMPORT CORP. P.O.BOX 1, BOSTON, USA	

Pre-Carrage by	⑥ Place of Receipt BUSAN, KOREA	
④ Ocean Vessel WONIS JIN	⑦ Voyage No. 1234E	⑫ Flag

⑤ Port of Loading BUSAN, KOREA	⑧ Port of Discharge BOSTON, USA	⑨ Place of Delivery BOSTON, USA	⑩ Final Destination(For the Merchant Ref.) BOSTON, USA

⑬ Container No. ⑭ Seal No. Marks & No	⑮ No. & Kinds of Containers or Packages	⑯ Description of Goods	⑰ Gross Weight	Measurement
ISCU1104	1 CNTR	LIGHT BULBS (64,000 PCS)	4,631 KGS	58,000 CBM
Total No. of Containers or Packages(in words)				

⑱ Freight and Charges	⑲ Revenue tons	⑳ Rate	㉑ Per	㉒ Prepaid	㉓ Collect

㉓ Freight prepaid at	㉔ Freight payable at	㉖ Place and Date of Issue May 21, 2022, Seoul Signature
Total prepaid in	㉕ No. of original B/L	
㉗ Laden on board vessel Date Signature May 21, 2022		㉘ ABC Shipping Co. Ltd. as agent for a carrier, zzz Liner Ltd.

[Model Letter 8-6: Sea Waybill(SWB)]

Non Negotiable Sea Waybill

Consignor(name, address, fax reference)	Shipper's reference Forwarder's reference	Bill of Lading number
	Unique consignment reference	
Consignee(name, address, fax reference)	Carrier(name, address, tax reference)	
Notify party(name, address, fax reference)	Additional notify party(name, address, fax reference)	

Pre-carriage by	Place of receipt	
Vessel/voyage no	Part of loading	
Part of discharge	Final place of delivery by on-carrier	

Marks and numbers; transport unit ID	Number and kind of packages; shipping description of goods	Gross weight	Measurement

Container no(s) Seal no(s)	Freight details, charge etc.	Rate	Per	Prepaid	Collect
	Freight payable at	Carrier's name			
	Number of original Bill of Lading	Place(+ISO code) and date of issue(yyy-mm-dd)			
Received for carriage as above in apparent good order and condition, unless otherwise stated hereon, The goods described in the above particulars		Authenticating Signature			

[Model Letter 8-7: Packing List]

PACKING LIST

<table>
<tr><td colspan="3">① Seller
Gil Dong Trading Co., Ltd.</td><td colspan="3">⑦ Invoice No. and date
8905 HC 3108 Aug. 15, 2022.</td></tr>
<tr><td colspan="3" rowspan="2">② Consignee(or For account & risk of Messrs.)
Monarch Products Co., Ltd.
P.O.Box 208
Bulawayo, Zimbabwe</td><td colspan="3">⑧ Buyer(if other than consignee)
Monarch Products Co., Ltd.
P.O.Box 208
Bulawayo, Zimbabwe</td></tr>
<tr><td colspan="3" rowspan="4">⑨ Other references
Country of Origin:
Republic of Korea</td></tr>
<tr><td colspan="3">③ Departure date
Aug. 20, 2022.</td></tr>
<tr><td colspan="2">④ Vessel/flight
Phoenix</td><td>⑤ From
BUSAN, KOREA</td></tr>
<tr><td colspan="3">⑥ To
Bulawayo, Zimbabwe</td></tr>
<tr><td>⑩ Shipping Marks</td><td>⑪ No.&kind of packages</td><td>⑫ Goods description</td><td>⑬ Quantity or net weight</td><td>⑭ Gross Weight</td><td>⑮ Measurement</td></tr>
<tr><td>MON/T
Bulawayo
LOT NO
C/NO.1-53
MADE IN KOREA</td><td>4200DX420D
Material,
As per Monarch
Products
Indent No T.858</td><td>Nylon Oxford</td><td>60,000M
1208.06Kgs.</td><td>1,317kgs</td><td>24.5CBM</td></tr>
<tr><td colspan="6">//</td></tr>
<tr><td colspan="4"></td><td colspan="2">Signed by
⑯</td></tr>
</table>

[Model Letter 8-8: Air Waybill(AWB)]

Shipper's Name and Address	Shipper's Account Number	Not negotiable **Air Waybill** *issued by* KOREAN AIR
		Copies 1, 2 and 3 of this Air Waybil are originals and have the same validity.
Consignee's Name and Address	Consignee's Account Number	It is agreed that the goods described herein are accepted in apparent good order and condition (except as noted) for carriage SUBJECT TO THE CONDITIONS OF CONTRACT ON THE REVERSE HEREOF. THE SHIPPER'S ATTENTION IS DRAWN TO THE NOTICE CONCERNING CARRIER'S LIMITATION OF LIABILITY. Shipper may increase such limitation of liability by declaring a higher value for carriage and paying a supplemental charge if required.
Telephone :		
Issuing Carrier's Agent Name and City		Accounting Information
Agent's IATA Code	Account No.	
Airport of Departure(Addr. of First Carrier) and Requested Routing		

TO	By First Carrier	Routing and Destination	to	by	to	by	Currency	CHGS Code	WT/VAL PPD	WT/VAL COLL	Other PPD	Other COLL	Declared Value for Carriage	Declared Value for Customs

Airport of Destination	Flight/Date	For Carrier Use Only	Flight/Date	Amount of Insurance	INSURANCE-If Carrier offers Insurance, and such insurance is requested in accordance with conditions on reverse hereof, indicate amount to be insured in figures in box marked 'amount of Insurance'.

Handling Information

No. of Pieces RCP	Gross Weight	kg lb	Rate Class / Commodity item No.	Chargeable Weight	Rate / Charge	Total	Nature and Quantity of Goods (incl. Dimensions or Volume)

Prepaid	Weight Charge	Collect	Other Charges
	Valuation Charge		
	Tax		
	Total Other Charges Due Agent		Shipper certifies that the particulars on the face hereof are correct and that insofar as any part of the consignment contalns dangerous goods, such part is properly described by name and is in proper condition for carriage by air according to the applicable Dangerous Goods Regulations.
	Total Other Charges Due Carrier		
			Signature of Shipper or his Agent
Total Prepaid		Total Collect	
Currency Conversion Rates		CC Charges In Dest. Currency	Executed on(date) at(place) Signature of Issuing Carrier or its Agent
For Carrier's Use Only at Destination		Charges at Destination	Total Collect Charges

ORIGINAL 3(FOR SHIPPER)

Key Expressions & Technical Terms

- ✔ **Air Waybill(AWB)**: Air waybill, a receipt issued by an international courier company. An air waybill(AWB) is a document that accompanies goods shipped by an international air courier to provide detailed information about the shipment and allow it to be tracked. An air waybill(AWB), also known as an air consignment note, is a type of bill of lading. However, an AWB serves a similar function to ocean bills of lading, but an AWB is issued in non-negotiable form, meaning there's less protection with an AWB versus bills of lading.

- ✔ **Bill of Lading(B/L)**: A bill of lading(sometimes abbreviated as B/L or BoL) is a document issued by a carrier which details a shipment of merchandise and gives title of that shipment to a specified party. Bills of lading are one of three important documents used in international trade to help guarantee that exporters receive payment and importers receive merchandise.

- ✔ **Conference Shipping**: Shipping conferences refers to shipping companies that have formed an association to agree on and set freight rates and passenger fares over different shipping routes. There are different shipping conferences for different regions of the world. Shipping conferences, aside from setting rates, adopt a wide number of policies such as allocation of customers, loyalty contracts, open pricing contracts, etc. Historically, eastern bloc country shipping lines have not joined these conferences.

- ✔ **Freight Collect**: used to state that the person or company that receives goods will pay the cost of transporting the goods at the time they are received: All freight and charges billed on a freight collect basis must be paid in full prior to release of the cargo.

✔ **Freight Prepaid**: A phrase typically used on a bill of lading to indicate that the cost of the goods' shipping has already been paid for and is not refundable. Many manufacturing businesses will ship their products freight prepaid to avoid having the intended receiver pay for shipping costs.

✔ **Inland Waterway Transport**: A body of water, such as a river, canal or lake, is navigable if it is deep, wide and slow enough for a vessel to pass or walk. Preferably there are few obstructions such as rocks or trees to avoid. Bridges must have sufficient clearance. High water speed may make a channel unnavigable. Waters may be unnavigable because of ice, particularly in winter. Navigability depends on context: A small river may be navigable by smaller craft, such as a motor boat or a kayak, but unnavigable by a cruise ship. Shallow rivers may be made navigable by the installation of locks that increase and regulate water depth, or by dredging.

✔ **liner/Tramp(er)**: A Tramper is UK Trucker slang for the driver or vehicle for long distance deliveries that may take several days. The vehicles themselves are large articulated lorries designed to allow the driver to sleep in overnight.

✔ **Packing List**: A shipping list, packing list, waybill, packing slip(also known as a bill of parcel, unpacking note, packaging slip, (delivery) docket, delivery list, manifest or customer receipt), is a shipping document that accompanies delivery packages, usually inside an attached shipping pouch or inside the package itself. It commonly includes an itemized detail of the package contents and does not include customer pricing. It serves to inform all parties, including transport agencies, government authorities, and customers, about the contents of the package. It helps them deal with the package accordingly.

✔ **Sea Waybill(SWB)**: A Sea Waybill is a transport contract(contract of carriage) - the same as a Bill of Lading. A Sea Waybill, however, is not needed for cargo delivery and is only issued as a cargo receipt. It can either be issued in hard copy format or soft copy format. A Sea Waybill is not negotiable and cannot be assigned to a third party.

✔ **Time Charter**: A time charter is a time-bound agreement, as opposed to a voyage charter. The shipowner leases a vessel to a charterer for a fixed period of time, and they are free to sail to any port and transport any cargo, subject to legal regulations.

✔ **Voyage Charter(Trip Charter)**: Chartering is an activity within the shipping industry. In some cases a charterer may own cargo and employ a shipbroker to find a ship to deliver the cargo for a certain price, called freight rate. Freight rates may be on a per-ton basis over a certain route (e.g. for iron ore between Brazil and China), in Worldscale points(in case of oil tankers) or alternatively may be expressed in terms of a total sum - normally in U.S. dollars - per day for the agreed duration of the charter.

Check-up Questions 08

Q1 Which one of the following is NOT a basic obligation for the seller as required by the contract during the Implementation Phase?

① Delivering the goods
② Handing over any documents relating to delivering and transferring the goods
③ Arranging financial documents or instruments for the payment
④ Handing over any documents relating to transferring the property in the goods

Q2 Which one is NOT considered a basic document required as per Transport Documents?

① Bill of Lading(B/L)
② Commercial Invoice
③ Packing List
④ Customs Invoice

Q3 Write the following sentence in English.

TK-1199A 형의 각종 주방기구 1,200대의 선적준비가 거의 다 되었습니다. 이에 선적지시를 이메일로 보내주시길 바랍니다. 귀사께서 즉시 동지해 주시면 선적일사를 3주간 단축할 수 있습니다.

[Useful expressions]

- a full range of kitchenware: 각종 주방기구
- be nearly ready for: 거의 다 되었다
- if you inform us at once: 즉시 통지해 주면
- the shipping date: 선적일자
- advance (shorten): 단축할 수 있다

➡

Q4 Write the following sentence in English.

4월 6일자 귀사의 전자우편을 받았으며, 불가항력의 사유로 인해 선적일자 3월 30일을 지킬 수 없게 되었음을 대단히 죄송하게 생각합니다. 이런 상황하에서 유감스럽지만 귀사의 주문 취소를 수락할 수밖에 없으나, 이 지연은 결코 당사의 잘못으로 야기된 것이 아님을 양해하여 주시기 바랍니다.

➡

Q5 Explain the following words and make a document.

① Air waybill(AWB)

② Bill of Lading(B/L)

③ Packing List

④ Sea Waybill(SWB)

9 CHAPTER

Global Business English

Implementation Phase: Marine Insurance

Chapter

9 Implementation Phase: Marine Insurance

Key Sentences

It can be tricky to decide if you need to take out marine cargo insurance. Weighing up the benefits and costs of taking out a policy varies with each business. The bottom line is that if you can't afford to replace your client's goods if they are lost or damaged, you need to take out the coverage.

Objectives

After studying this lesson, you will be able to:

- understand marine insurance in the implementation phase of the contract
- identify the concept and contents of marine insurance
- interpret insurance documents

해상보험(marine insurance)이란 해상위험에 의해 발생하는 손해를 보상할 것을 목적으로 하는 보험으로서 손해보험의 일종이다. 영국 해상보험법(Marine Insurance Act 1906: MIA) 제1조에서는 "해상보험계약은 보험자가 피보험자에 대하여 그 계약에 의해 합의된 방법과 범위 내에서 해상손해, 즉 해상사업에 수반되는 손해를 보상할 것을 확약하는 계약"이라고 정의하고 있다.

해상보험은 보험의 목적물에 따라 여러 가지로 나눌 수 있지만, 그중에서도 적하보험(cargo insurance)과 선박보험(hull insurance)이 중심이 된다. 물품을 대상으로 하는 무역거래에서는 적화물에 대하여 보험에 부보함으로써 해상위험으로부터 발생하는 손해를 줄이고 무역거래의 원활을 도모할 수 있다.

보험서류(insurance documents)란 무역물품의 운송 도중 해난이나 기타의 위험으로 인하여 입게 될 손해에 대하여 보험을 부보하고 이에 대하여 보험자로부터 발급받는 증거서류를 말한다. CIF와 CIP 매매계약에서는 매도인이 적하보험을 부보하고 이에 대한 보험서류를 매수인에게 제공할 의무가 있다.

신용장거래에서는 해상적하보험의 성립을 증명하는 서류를 총칭하여 보험서류라고 하는데, 이에는 보험증권(Insurance Policy: I/P), 보험증명서(insurance certificate), 통지서(declaration)가 있다.

9-1 Fundamental Concepts and Types of Marine Insurance

1. What is marine insurance?

A contract of marine insurance is a contract whereby the insurer undertakes to indemnify the assured, in manner and to the extent thereby agreed, against marine losses, that is to say, the losses incident to marine adventure(MIA 1906). Marine insurance protects you against potential financial exposure arising from physical damage or losses to goods while being transported worldwide. Although the term "marine" might make you instantly think of sea transport, the coverage expands to any goods in transit by road, rail, sea, or air.

In the GBT, goods travel long distances to another country. Both the exporter and the importer face all kinds of possible risks or losses all the time, and therefore goods must be insured against loss or damage at each stage of their journey. In other words, no matter what means of transport is being used, insurance exists to protect the importer or exporter against the possible financial losses which he/she would otherwise suffer in case damage or loss was inflicted upon him/her. Without adequate insurance and protection of the interests of those with goods in transit, the global business transaction cannot be guaranteed.

2. What are the types of marine insurance?

There are four types of marine insurance.
Marine cargo insurance protects goods during loading and unloading, storage, and transportation. This can include protection against loss or damage to the goods, as well as against liability for any damage that the goods may cause to third parties. Cargo insurance can be purchased by the shipper or the carrier, and the terms of the policy will vary depending on who purchases it.

Hull Insurance is insurance for ships that carry goods. It covers all kinds of vessels going into the ocean, like ships, pontoons, yachts, cruises tankers, bulk carrier, dredgers, trawlers, fishing boats and other pleasure boats, jetties and wharfs.

Freight insurance is vital for companies that rely on the transport of goods to conduct their business. It protects against the loss or damage of goods in transit, whether by land, sea, or air. If goods are lost or damaged, freight insurance can reimburse the company for the cost of the goods, as well as any associated expenses such as transport and storage. It can also cover the company for the loss of revenue if the goods are not able to be delivered to the customer.

Liability insurance is a type of marine insurance where compensation is sought to be provided to any liability occurring on account of a ship colliding or crashing and on account of any other induced attacks.

9-2 Parties and Necessity of Marine Insurance

1. Who is marine cargo insurance for?

Marine cargo insurance is essential for small and large businesses that import, export, or distribute goods around the UK and the wider world. According to the Marine Insurance Act 1906(MIA 1906), any company with an "insurable interest" can take out marine cargo insurance.

The insurable interest covers raw materials, finished products, general merchandise, machinery, and appliances. Therefore, manufacturers, merchants, wholesalers, retailers, and distributors all have an insurable interest and should all be aware of marine cargo insurance and its protection relative to the entire marine insurance market.

2. Why do I need marine insurance?

Although marine insurance is often considered unnecessary, the cover can protect all interested parties from expensive burdens when things go wrong.

Hauliers typically don't insure cargo individually. Instead, they acquire a marine policy that only covers their liability for loss or damage to goods. Even if they are liable in the event of loss or damage to goods, their contract conditions typically result in clients only being able to reclaim a fraction of the actual cost of the goods.

9-3 The Contents of a Marine Cargo Insurance Policy*

1. What does marine insurance cover?

Typically, the insurance covers the loss or damage to property caused due to.

- Natural disasters
- Man-made disasters such as theft and piracy
- Collision or derailment of land transit
- Incidents related to ships such as sinking or stranding
- The loading and unloading of cargo
- Storage in warehouses between transit stages for up to 60 days
- Incurred expenses such as survey fees and reconditioning costs
- Maritime principles such as General Average

The coverage varies across policies, and there are several clauses to be aware of. There are three main types of Institute Cargo Clauses, A, B, and C, spanning different levels of coverage from the list above.

In fact, there are over 150 other Institute Clauses tailored to meet the needs of specific trades. You can usually find a complete list of all clauses in the policy documentation.

2. What is not covered under Marine Insurance?

There are also some things to be aware of that aren't covered and can affect your liability. These include the loss or damage to property caused by.

- Insecure packaging by suppliers for the method of transport used
- Intentional damage or misconduct

* https://www.letsbloom.com/blog/marine-insurance/

- Spoilage due to the product's nature - such as perishables and combustible substances
- Dangerous goods such as firearms and ammunition
- Shipping delays resulting in deterioration of goods
- Ordinary wear and tear
- Riots, strikes, or war
- The financial default of the owners or operators of the vessel

9-4 Procedures of Marine Cargo Insurance

In export trade, who will effect insurance depends on the particular trade terms adopted. Under CIF terms, it is the seller who arranges insurance with an insurance company; under the terms as FOB, CFR, the buyer effects insurance, but he/she may ask the seller to arrange insurance on behalf of the buyer. They may start by inquiring and choosing the right coverage and then negotiate insurance premium rates. Sometimes, brokers may be used whose assistance can be of enormous benefit as they are highly skilled specialists and can obtain sound and reliable coverage, together with competitive premium rates. An insurance policy is issued when goods are insured, but it is also usual for a certificate of insurance to be issued for documentary purposes. In completing the insurance contract, either party, buyer or seller will undergo the following different steps.

1. To Apply for Marine Insurance

In some countries, the first step the insured party should take is to apply for insurance from a certain insurance company. The applicant should fill in the special form or the proposal form, which gives all the details concerning ownership, value, time span insurance will be for, risk and coverage, etc.

2. To determine the Insurance Value for the Good to Be Insured

The value to be insured is measured on the value of the commercial invoice; the recommended minimum amount is the total CIF value plus 10% for other fees and normal margin of profit. Probably the best way of determining the needed insurance is to estimate the market value of the goods at the port of destination and to obtain coverage for that amount. Other approaches to evaluate the goods may also be agreed upon by the insurer and insured to meet individual needs. The calculation and determination of the value to be insured vary from country to country.

3. To Determine the Insurance Average and Coverage

Determination of the right coverage sometimes can be made only on the basis of the following factors: the nature of the product, packing considerations such as sacks or paper boxes; use of the products such as chemicals or tea; the carriers of the transport such as the difference of air and sea transport, shipping route and ports considerations such as any transhipment on the way to the final port, etc.

4. To Determine Insurance Premium Rates

The rates charged by the insurance company are based on such factors as the type of coverage desired, shipping routes, modes of transport, duration of the voyage, and nature of the goods and packing. Also important is each shipper's past loss experience. After a period of favourable experience, rates may be lowered. Conversely, a shipper with a bad loss record may find his/her premium increased. Generally, the greater the risks that the consignment is exposed to, the higher the premium will be.

5. To Sign an Insurance Policy

Before filling in and signing an insurance policy, it is essential to have a good understanding about what an insurance policy is, and the kind of insurance policies. The most extensively used policies now in the international trade, which are insurance policy, insurance certificate and open policy. As far as the details of these documents are concerned, please refer to the "*Fundamental Concepts*" section of this Unit.

6. To Lodge an Insurance Claim

Whenever an actual loss occurs, claims can be made by the shipper, the buyer or even a carrier that has first lien on goods. It is of vital importance that the insured must be able to prove a loss by perils against which he/she was insured. The one who registers a claim should get the survey report conducted by the expert, together with a copy of the bill of lading, the commercial invoice, the insurance policy, and a covering letter requesting payment, and then send them to the insurance company for processing.

Most insurance company policies require that immediate notice be given to the nearest branch or agency in the event of damage giving rise to a claim. This notice means that a claim has been filed. A delay in giving the notice might result in the underwriter's refusal to process the claim. When notified of damage, the insurance company will appoint a suitable surveyor to inspect the goods and to report on the nature and extent of the damage. As a common practice, a report or certificate of loss together with the surveyor's findings will be issued to the consignees, who pay the fee. This certificate of loss is included with the claim papers and, if the loss is recoverable under the insurance cover, the fee is refunded to the claimants.

In some circumstances, the claim papers are returned to the place where the insurance was carried out and subsequently to the underwriters. However, especially where goods are sold on CIF terms and the policy is assigned to the consignee; arrangements are made for any claims to be paid at the destination. In such cases, the consignees approach the agents named in the policy for payment of their claims. Of course, the claims procedure will vary by circumstances, but undoubtedly a quicker settlement should be secured in the event of loss or damage. As a matter of fact, settling a claim is not so easy; it needs patience, evidence and knowledge.

9-5 Model Letter of Marine Insurance

[Model Letter 9–1: Insurance Coverage Request]

Gentlemen:

We have received your facsimile of December 12 regarding marine insurance for your order No. M0-001.

As this contract is on an F.O.B basis, marine insurance on the consignments should be effected by you. The present shipping schedule is that the shipments of 70 units for ₩14,000,000 are to be loaded on the Gloria due to leave Inchŏn port on or about December 21. The shipping advice will be given to you by teletransmission as soon as the shipment has been finished. The remainder of 30 units for ₩6,000,000 will be scheduled in January.

We assure you that we will take special note of your shipping instructions.

Very truly yours,

[Model Letter 9-2: Insurance Contract Application]

The Star Marine Insurance Co., Ltd.

Gentlemen:

This is to confirm our instruction via telephone yesterday. as per copy enclosed, we shall be pleased of you will effect insurance for us subject to ICC(B) on U.S. $10,000.00 value of 100cases canned provisions, to be shipped from Pusan on the S.S HANBADA, sailing for Los Angeles on or about July 25, 2022.

Would you please send us the insurance policy, together with the statement of premium due soon.

Your prompt attention to this matter would be much appreciated.

Very truly yours,

[Model Letter 9-3: Notice of Insurance Coverage]

Gentlemen:

we have received with thanks The Hanvit Bank Letter of Credit No. 23568 Covering your Order No. 160, and are glad to note that everything stipulated therein is quite all right except that your buyer specified that insurance is to be against ICC(A). You will doubtless recall that there is an understanding between you and us that we quote CIF prices on the basis of ICC(B), with additional clauses for the buyer's account. This means that ICC(A), War Risk, and S.R & C.C. Risks are to be borne by the buyer.

In this instance, we will absorb the difference between ICC(B) and ICC(A), but from now on please do not fail to insert a notation on your sales note that any additional coverage other than ICC(B) shall be for the account of the buyer.

Thank you.

Very truly yours,

[Model Letter 9-4: ICC(B) Insurance Premium Inquiry]

Gentlemen:

Please quote us your rate for Marine Insurance, ICC(B) including war risk, on a shipment of 10 cases of cotton goods, valued at ₩300,000 by the s/s "Arirang" from Pusan to Hong Kong.

The ship will sail from Pusan on 2nd September, and we hope to have your reply by return.

Your truly,

[Model Letter 9-5: Reply to Insurance Premium Inquiry]

Gentlemen:

In response to your inquiry of 27th of this month, we wish to quote you the rate of Marine Insurance at 0.315 percent, ICC(B) including war risk, on the shipment referred to in your letter.

This is exceptionally low rate, because many of the insurance companies will hesitate to take the risk at any premium whatever dreading the heavy average to which they are exposed on the South China Sea.

We hope that you will pass us your business.

Yours very truly,

[Model Letter 9-6: Insurance Payment Notice]

Gentlemen:

We are pleased to receive your letter of May 26, regarding 600 bags damaged Rice by s.s "Arirang." We have pleasure in enclosing you a check for ₩108,000 in settlement of your claim. We shall be glad to have your receipt in due course.

Yours very truly,

9-6 Marine Insurance Documents

The cargo insurance document is a contact whereby the insurer(insurance company), on the basis of a premium paid, undertakes to indemnify the insured against loss from certain risks or perils to which the cargo insured may be exposed. It is an indispensable adjunct of international trade. Without adequate insurance and protection of the interests of those with goods in transit, international trade cannot be guaranteed. Whether the responsibility for shipment insurance provision is the buyer's or the seller's is decided according to the details of the particular export sales contract. The following are the important insurance documents.

- Insurance Policy
- Insurance Certificate
- Insurance Declaration
- Cover Note

1. Insurance Policy

Broadly, an insurance policy is the entire written contract of insurance. It provides actionable evidence of an insurance contract. More specifically, it is the basic written or printed document, as well as the coverage forms and endorsement added to it. A typical insurance policy should include the following data.

- Name, address and signature of the insurer
- Name of the insured
- The endorsement of the insured
- A description of the risks covered and the insured time
- Description of consignment
- The sum or sums insured
- Premium

2. Insurance Certificate

An insurance certificate is a document indicating the type and amount of insurance coverage in force on a particular shipment, used to assure the consignee that insurance is provided to cover loss of or damage of the cargo while in transit.

In some cases, a shipper may issue a document that certifies that a shipment has been insured under a given open policy, and that the certificate represents and takes the place of such an open policy, the provisions of which are controlling. In many countries, it is not actionable.

3. Insurance Declaration

A declaration, in the context of insurance, is the first page or pages of a liability or property insurance policy that contains factual information about the policyholder, the property (in property insurance policies) or items covered, and other important information about the policy. An insurance declaration page also known as a "dec page" summarizes the insurance coverage provided by the policy.

4. Cover Note

A cover note is a temporary certificate of insurance issued by the Insurer before the issuance of a policy after the Insured has given a duly filled in proposal form and has paid the premium in full.

[Model Letter 9-7: Insurance Certificate]

LG Insurance Co., Ltd.

CERTIFICATE OF MARINE CARGO INSURANCE

<table>
<tr><td colspan="3">Assured(s), etc ② THE SAMWON CORPORATION</td></tr>
<tr><td colspan="2">Certificate No.
① 002599A65334</td><td>Ref. No.③ Invoice No. DS-990228
L/C No. IOMP20748</td></tr>
<tr><td colspan="2">Claim, if any, payable at : ⑥
GELLATLY HANKEY MARINE SERVICE
842 Seventh Avenue New York 10018
Tel(201)881-9412
Claims are payable in</td><td>Amount insured ④
USD 65,120.-
(USD59,200 XC 110%)</td></tr>
<tr><td colspan="2">Survey should be approved by ⑦
THE SAME AS ABOVE</td><td rowspan="5">Conditions ⑤
* INSTITUTE CARGO CLAUSE(A) 1982
* CLAIMS ARE PAYABLE IN AMERICA IN THE CURRENCY OF THE DRAFT.</td></tr>
<tr><td>⑧ Local Vessel or Conveyance</td><td>⑨From(interior port or place of loading)</td></tr>
<tr><td>Ship or Vessel called the
⑩ KAJA-HO V-27</td><td>Sailing on or about
⑪ MARCH 3, 2013</td></tr>
<tr><td>at and from
⑫ BUSAN, KOREA</td><td>⑬ transshipped at</td></tr>
<tr><td>arrived at
⑭NEW YORK</td><td>⑮ thence to</td></tr>
<tr><td colspan="2">Goods and Merchandises ⑯
16,000YDS OF PATCHWORK COWHIDE LEATHER</td><td>Subject to the following Clauses as per back hereof institute Cargo Clauses Institute War Clauses(Cargo)
Institute War Cancellation Clauses(Cargo)
Institute Strikes Riots and Civil Commotions Clauses
Institute Air Cargo Clauses(All Risks)
Institute Classification Clauses
Special Replacement Clause(applying to machinery)
Institute Radioactive Contamination Exclusion Clauses
Co-Insurance Clause Marks and Numbers as</td></tr>
<tr><td colspan="3">Place and Date signed in ⑰ SEOUL, KOREA MARCH 2, 2013 No. of Certificates issued. ⑱ TWO
⑳ This Certificate represents and takes the place of the Policy and conveys all rights of the original policyholder (for the purpose of collecting any loss or claim) as fully as if the property was covered by a Open Policy direct to the holder of this Certificate.
This Company agrees losses, if any, shall be payable to the order of Assured on surrender of this Certificate.
Settlement under one copy shall render all others null and void.
Contrary to the wording of this form, this insurance is governed by the standard from of English Marine Insurance Policy.
In the event of loss or damage arising under this insurance, no claims will be admitted unless a survey has been held with the approval of this Company's office or Agents specified in this Certificate.

SEE IMPORTANT INSTRUCTIONS ON REVERSE
⑲ LG Insurance Co., Ltd.

AUTHORIZED SIGNATORY

This Certificate is not valid unless the Declaration be signed by an authorized representative of the Assured.</td></tr>
</table>

[Model Letter 9-8: Insurance Policy - Sample Pages(out of 60)]

〈Front Cover〉

CNA

250 Yonge Street, 15th Floor
Toronto, Ontario M5B 2L7
Telephone: 416-542-7300
Fax: 416-542-7410
Toll Free: 1-800-268-939

MARINE
CARGO POLICY

POLICY No:

PLEASE READ THIS POLICY (AND THE DECLARATION PAGE(S) WHICH FORMS AN INTEGRAL PART OF THE POLICY). IF IT DOES NOT MEET WITH YOUR REQUIREMENTS YOU SHOULD INFORM US IMMEDIATELY THROUGH YOUR INSURANCE BROKER

Continental Casualty Company (hereinafter referred to as the **Insurer**) and the **Insured** agree that in consideration of the premium paid to the **Insurer,** the **Insurer** will insure the cargo against direct physical loss or damage in accordance with the terms and conditions of this policy for the Policy Period shown.

The declaration pages, wording, and exclusions incorporate terms and conditions which may limit cover or, in certain situations, exclude cover, in addition to the Policy Terms and Conditions and Endorsements which also contain limits in cover and exclusions.

Words set out in **bold** have the meaning set out in the definitions section, wherever they appear in the policy.

This policy shall not be in force unless countersigned by an authorized representative of the Continental Casualty Company.

Countersigned at this day of

INITIAL

CHIEF AGENT FOR CANADA

〈Page 2 of 60〉

PART B: POLICY OF INSURANCE TERMS AND CONDITIONS

1. Definitions

The following expressions shall have the meanings set out below wherever they appear in bold in the **Policy**:

"Insured" or "Assured" means the individual, partnership, corporation or other entity named in the declaration pages, and consignees as determined by terms of sale of the goods, and if they have an insurable interest in the cargo.

"Insurer" or "Insurers" means Continental Casualty Company

"Policy" means, collectively, Part A: Declaration Page (including any declaration page issued in substitution), Part B: Policy of Insurance Terms Conditions, Part C: Additional Clauses and Part D: Endorsements attached thereto.

"Underwriter" or "Underwriters" means Continental Casualty Company

2. Insured

The **Insured** named on the Declaration page shall be entitled to the benefit of this **Policy** provided the **Insured** has an insurable interest in the cargo at the time of the loss.

3. Period of Attachment

This **Policy** shall cover and attach on all shipments made on or after 12:01 a.m. local standard time at place of issue of this **Policy** and prior to date of expiry or cancellation of this **Policy.**

4. Subject Matter Insured

This **Policy** shall only cover new and similar goods, as set out on the Declaration Page(s), incidental to the **Insured's** normal business, suitably packed for transit.

5. Cancellation

This **Policy** may be cancelled by either **Underwriters** or the **Assured** giving thirty days notice in writing to take effect from midnight of the day notice of cancellation is issued, but such cancellation shall not prejudice any risk or risks which shall have already attached.

Cancellation of War, Strikes, Riots and Civil Commotions and Malicious Damage Risks provided, as outlined in the War Risk Clause and the Strikes, Riots, Civil Commotions, Etc. Clause is as set out in paragraph 12.9.

CNA

6. Limits of Liability

The **Insurers** shall not be liable for more than the amounts as set out on the Declaration Page(s)

If the total value at risk exceeds the limit(s) of liability provided by this **Policy**, the Insured shall nevertheless report the full amount at risk to the **Insurers** and shall pay full premium thereon. Acceptance of such reports and premium shall not alter or increase the limit(s) of liability of the **Insurers**, but **Insurers** shall be liable for the full amount of coverage up to, but not exceeding, the applicable limit(s) of liability.

The limit of liability of the **Insurer** with respect to the coverages provided for in the General Average and/or Salvage Charges and/or Special Charges shall not be separate from, or in addition to, the limit of liability set forth above and shall not be separate from or in addition to any other limit(s) of liability set forth in this **Policy**.

The limit of liability of the **Insurer** with respect to the coverage provided for sue and labour shall not exceed fifty (50) percent of the limit of liability in Part A of this policy. For greater clarification, where the relevant limit is set out in an applicable additional clause or in the sub limits set out in paragraphs 1-55, then the sue and labour limit shall be fifty (50) percent of the applicable additional clause limit or sub limit.

7. Accumulation Clause

The limits of liability expressed herein shall not apply in the event of or during transhipment or after the arrival of the overseas vessel or conveyance at the port or place of discharge, provided always that any accumulation of goods during the ordinary course of transit beyond such limits of liability shall not have arisen from circumstances within the control of the **Assured**. Should there be any other accumulation of goods beyond such limits of liability by reason of interruption of transit and/or other circumstances beyond the control of the **Assured**, **Insurers** shall, provided notice be given in all such cases as soon as known to the **Assured**, hold covered such excess amount and be liable for the full amount at risk.

In no event shall **Underwriters** be liable hereunder for more than double the limits of liability expressed herein or $5,000,000, whichever is the less, unless increased with prior agreement of **Underwriters**.

Key Expressions & Technical Terms

✔ **Actual Total Loss/Constructive Total Loss**: These two terms are used to differentiate the degree of proof where a vessel or cargo has been lost. An actual total loss occurs where the damages or cost of repair clearly equal or exceed the value of the property. A constructive total loss is a situation where the cost of repairs plus the cost of salvage equal or exceed the value. The use of these terms is contingent on there being property remaining to assess damages, which is not always possible in losses to ships at sea or in total theft situations. In this respect, marine insurance differs from non-marine insurance, where the insured is required to prove his loss. Traditionally, in law, marine insurance was seen as an insurance of "the adventure", with insurers having a stake and an interest in the vessel and/or the cargo rather than simply an interest in the financial consequences of the subject-matter's survival.

✔ **FPA(Free from Particular Average)**: Marine insurance provision which limits the liability of an insurance company to only those losses that exceed a specified percentage of the value of the goods. It is similar to the deductible clause included in other types of insurance, but is not applicable where a cover for total loss is in force. FPA conditions are applied where the goods are extremely susceptible to damage, or are rendered almost worthless from exposure to water or heat. However, its usage differs in the UK(where it applies to partial loss caused directly or indirectly by mishaps such as burning, collision, sinking, or stranding of the ship) from its usage in the US(where it applies only to loss caused directly by such mishaps). The broker had to decide whether the raisins were fair average quality from foreign competition.

✔ **Fresh Water Rain Damage**: Water damage describes a large number of possible losses caused by water intruding where it will enable attack of a material or system by destructive processes such as rotting of wood, growth, rusting of steel, de-laminating of materials such as plywood, and many others.

✔ **Insurance Coverage**: The amount of risk or liability covered for an individual or entity by way of insurance services. Insurance coverage is issued by an insurer in the event of an unforeseen or unwanted occurrences. There are general different types of insurance coverage, such as auto or life or more exotic forms such as hole-in-one insurance.

✔ **Insurance Policy/Certificate**: In insurance, the insurance policy is a contract(generally a standard form contract) between the insurer and the insured, known as the policyholder, which determines the claims which the insurer is legally required to pay. In exchange for an initial payment, known as the premium, the insurer promises to pay for loss caused by perils covered under the policy language.

✔ **Insured Amount(Value)/Premium**: Amount for which an insurance cover is bought on a building, and the basis on which insurance premium is computed. According to the coinsurance clause, it must not be lower than a certain percentage(usually 80 percent) of the insurable value of the building to be able to claim a partial loss in full.

✔ **Leakage/Spillage**: Leakage(chemistry), a process in which material is lost through holes or defects of their containers.

✔ **Particular Average**: Marine insurance provision under which damages or expenses incurred by a shipper(whose cargo is exposed to a danger) are borne by that shipper only. Such damages or expenses occur by direct harm to the ship and/or cargo, or in a course of action to prevent initial or additional harm to them. Particular average, like general-average is independent of the insurance cover bought for the cargo. Instead, it arises out of the contract between the cargo-owner and the ship-owner. Now largely replaced by the relevant institute cargo clause.

✔ **Pilferage**: Pilferage is the theft of part of the contents of a package. It may also include theft of the contents but leaving the package, perhaps resealed with bogus contents. Small packages can be pilfered from a larger package such as a shipping container. Broader and related aspects of theft may include taking the entire package, pallet load, truck load, shoplifting, etc.

✔ **Total Loss/Partial Loss**: In insurance, a total loss or write–off is a judgment, by the insurer, that the lost value or repair cost of a damaged property exceeds the value of its policy, resulting in what it concludes is a "total loss" or "constructive total loss" A constructive total loss factors other incidental expenses beyond repair, such as salvage. Policies covering homes, vehicles and other non-investment assets subject to depreciation typically pay the insured only a fraction of the cost of replacing the property, meaning they could become "total losses" even though some value remains. About one in seven car accident claims results in a "total."

✔ **Underwriter**: In insurance, underwriting is to sign and accept liability and guaranteeing payment in case loss or damage occurs. Underwriting is provided by a large financial service provider such as a bank, insurer or investment house.

Check-up Questions 09

Q1 Translate the following sentence in Korean.

No matter what means of transport is being used, insurance exists to protect the importer or exporter against the possible financial losses which he/she would otherwise suffer in case damage or loss was inflicted upon him/her. Without adequate insurance and protection of the interests of those with goods in transit, the global business transaction cannot be guaranteed.

➥

Q2 Translate the following sentence in Korean.

In export trade, who will effect insurance depends on the particular trade terms adopted. Under CIF terms, it is the seller who arranges insurance with an insurance company; under the terms as FOB, CFR, the buyer effects insurance, but he/she may ask the seller to arrange insurance on behalf of the buyer.

➥

Q3 Write the following sentence in English.

이 계약은 F.O.B 기준이므로 화물에 대한 해상보험은 귀사가 이행해야 합니다. 현재 선적 일정은 12월 21일경 인천항을 출항하기 때문에 글로리아호에 70개 1,400만원 선적 예정입니다.

➥

Q4 Write the following sentence in English.

이 경우 ICC(B)와 ICC(A)의 차액은 당사가 부담하지만, 앞으로는 ICC(B) 이외의 추가 보장은 구매자가 부담해야 한다는 것임을 귀사의 판매계약서에 반드시 기재하십시오.

➥

Q5 Explain the following words and make a document.

① Insurance Policy

② Insurance Certificate

③ Insurance Declaration

④ Cover Note

10 CHAPTER

Global Business English

Implementation Phase: International Payment

Chapter

10 Implementation Phase: International Payment

Key Sentences

Don't lose potential business to competitors by overlooking different payment options which could be attractive to your international buyer. Explore several payment methods and find the one best suited to your needs.

Objectives

After studying this lesson, you will be able to:

- understand the payment in the implementation phase of the contract
- identify methods and contents of International payment

매매당사자는 물품매매계약을 체결할 때 대금결제조건(payment terms)으로 ① 대금결제의 방식, ② 대금결제의 시기, ③ 결제통화 등에 대하여 약정하여야 한다.

무역대금의 결제방식으로는 신용장방식(L/C basis)에 의한 결제, 추심방식(collection basis)에 의한 결제 및 송금방식(remittance basis)에 의한 결제로 크게 구분할 수 있는데, 이 중 신용장방식에 의한 결제가 가장 보편적인 방식이다.

대금결제의 시기로 선지급조건(advance payment)은 수출입대금을 물품의 선적 또는 인도 이전에 미리 결제하는 방식으로 견본 구입이나 소액거래에서 사용된다. 동시지급조건(concurrent payment)은 현물 또는 현물을 화체한 서류(B/L 등)의 인도와 상환으로 대금결제가 이루어진다. 후지급조건(연지급: deferred payment)은 물품의 선적 또는 인도나 선적서류의 인도가 있은 후 일정기간이 경과되어야 대금결제가 이루어지는 외상거래조건으로 수출자에게 불리하며, 본지사 간 거래, 선박·플랜트 수출에 주로 이용된다.

무역매매가격의 산출 시에 통화는 어느 국가의 통화로 할 것인가를 약정하여야 한다. 보통 품목(commodity), 수량(quantity), 단가(unit price), 금액(amount)이 명시될 때에는 단가와 금액란에 "@US$5.30, US$53,000"과 같이 각각 표시하면 되지만, 결제조건(payment terms)을 언급할 때는 "Payment Terms: Under T/T basis in U.S. Dollars"와 같이 결제통화를 명시하여야 한다.

10-1 Payment Instruments of GBT

As we have learned earlier, financial documents, also called instruments, are widely used in international trade and payment. They clearly record currency to a certain extent, circulating among participants, facilitating the transfer of credits, acting as payment and credit tools in merchandise exchange. In GBT, the main instruments of payment are the currency and bills, i.e. bill of exchange(draft).

The bill of exchange or draft has played a vital part in the world's commercial and financial life for some countries. Also, it is widely used for settlement in international trade. A bill of exchange or draft is an unconditional order in writing prepared by one party(drawer) and addressed to another(drawee) directing the drawee to pay a specialised sum of money to the order of a third person(the payee), or to the bearer, on demand or at a fixed and determinable future time.

In conjunction with the definition, Figure 10-1 Specimen: Bill of Lading may be dissected as follows.

① An unconditional order in writing
② Addressed by one person/party(the drawer)
③ To another (the drawee)
④ Signed by the person (the drawer) giving it
⑤ Requiring the person to whom it is addressed (the drawee or payor) to pay

⑥ On demand, or at a fixed or determinable future time

⑦ A certain sum of money

⑧ To, or to the order of, a specified person, or to the bearer(the payee)

[Figure 10-1] Specimen: Bill of Exchange

Bill of Exchange

London, 31 January 2000 Amount US$ 250,000

At 60 days after sight pay against this Sole Bill of Exchange

to the order of Ourselves

the sum of US Dollars Two hundred and fifty thousand

for value Received

To:
Singapore Import Banking Company
Bank Street
Singapore

Drawn under UK Export Banking Company Ltd, Documentary Credit Nº 12345, Dated 29 September 1999

For and on behalf of:
UK Export Company Ltd

Jas. Smith

James Smith, Director

10-2 Methods of Payment

To succeed in today's global marketplace and win sales against foreign competitors, exporters must offer their customers attractive sales terms supported by the appropriate payment methods. Because getting paid in full and on time is the ultimate goal for each export sale, an appropriate payment method must be chosen carefully to minimize the payment risk while also accommodating the needs of the buyer. As shown in figure 10-2, there are five primary methods of payment for international transactions. During or before contract negotiations, you should consider which method in the figure is mutually desirable for you and your customer.

[Figure 10-2] Payment Risk Diagram

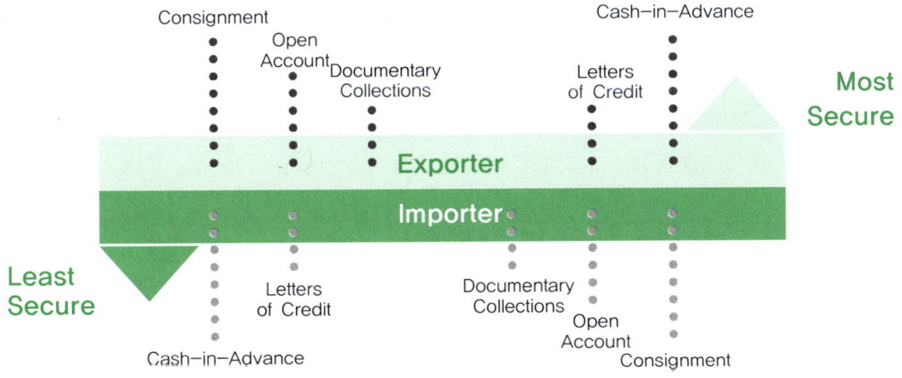

출처: https://www.trade.gov/methods-payment(2023.08.02.)

1. Cash-in-Advance

With cash-in-advance payment terms, an exporter can avoid credit risk because payment is received before the ownership of the goods is transferred. For international sales, wire transfers and credit cards are the most commonly used cash-in-advance options available to exporters. With the advancement of the Internet, escrow services are becoming another cash–in–advance option for small export transactions. However, requiring payment in advance is the least attractive option for the buyer, because it creates unfavorable cash flow. Foreign buyers are also concerned that the goods may not be sent if payment is made in advance. Thus, exporters who insist on this payment method as their sole manner of doing business may lose to competitors who offer more attractive payment terms. Learn more about Cash-in-Advance.

2. Documentary Collections

A documentary collection(D/C) is a transaction whereby the exporter entrusts the collection of the payment for a sale to its bank(remitting bank), which sends the documents that its buyer needs to the importer's bank(collecting bank), with instructions to release the documents to the buyer for payment. Funds are received from the importer and remitted to the exporter through the banks involved in the collection in exchange for those documents. D/Cs involve using a draft that requires the importer to pay the face amount either at sight(document against payment) or on a specified date(document against acceptance). The collection letter gives instructions that specify the documents required for the transfer of title to the goods. Although banks do act as facilitators for their clients, D/Cs offer no verification process and limited recourse in the event of non-payment. D/Cs are generally less expensive than LCs.

3. Open Account

An open account transaction is a sale where the goods are shipped and delivered before payment is due, which in international sales is typically in 30, 60 or 90 days. Obviously, this is one of the most advantageous options to the importer in terms of cash flow and cost, but it is consequently one of the highest risk options for an exporter. Because of intense competition in export markets, foreign buyers often press exporters for open account terms since the extension of credit by the seller to the buyer is more common abroad. Therefore, exporters who are reluctant to extend credit may lose a sale to their competitors. Exporters can offer competitive open account terms while substantially mitigating the risk of non–payment by using one or more of the appropriate trade finance techniques covered later in this Guide. When offering open account terms, the exporter can seek extra protection using export credit insurance.

4. Consignment

Consignment in international trade is a variation of open account in which payment is sent to the exporter only after the goods have been sold by the foreign distributor to the end customer. An international consignment transaction is based on a contractual arrangement in which the foreign distributor receives, manages, and sells the goods for the exporter who retains title to the goods until they are sold. Clearly, exporting on consignment is very risky as the exporter is not guaranteed any payment and its goods are in a foreign country in the hands of an independent distributor or agent. Consignment helps exporters become more competitive on the basis of better availability and faster delivery of goods. Selling on consignment can also help exporters reduce the direct costs of storing and managing inventory. The key to success in exporting on consignment is to partner with a reputable and trustworthy foreign distributor or a third-party logistics provider. Appropriate insurance should be in place to cover consigned goods in transit or in possession of a foreign distributor as well as to mitigate the risk of non-payment.

5. Letters of Credit(L/C)

A letter of credit(L/C) adds a bank's promise to pay the exporter to that of the foreign buyer provided that the exporter has complied with all the terms and conditions of the L/C. The foreign buyer applies for issuance of a L/C from the buyer's bank to the exporter's bank and therefore is called the applicant; the exporter is called the beneficiary.

Payment under a documentary letter of credit is based on documents, not on the terms of sale or the physical condition of the goods. The L/C specifies the documents that are required to be presented by the exporter, such as an ocean B/L (original and several copies), consular invoice, draft, and an insurance policy. The L/C also contains an expiration date. Before payment, the bank responsible for making payment, verifies that all documents conform to the L/C requirements. If not, the discrepancy must be resolved before payment can be made and before the expiration date.

An L/C issued by a foreign bank is sometimes confirmed by a Korean bank. This confirmation means that the Korean bank(the confirming bank), adds its promise to pay to that of the foreign bank(the issuing bank). If an L/C is not confirmed, it is advised through a Korean bank and thus called an advised L/C. Korean exporters may wish to confirm the L/C issued by foreign banks if they are unfamiliar with the foreign banks or concerned about the political or economic risk associated with the country in which the bank is located. An Export Assistance Center or international banker can assist exporters in evaluating the risks to determine what might be appropriate for specific export transactions.

An L/C may either be irrevocable and thus, unable to be changed unless both parties agree; or revocable where either party may unilaterally make changes. A revocable L/C is inadvisable as it carries many risks for the exporter.

A change made to a letter of credit after it has been issued is called an amendment. Banks also charge fees for this service. It should be specified in the amendment if the exporter or the buyer will pay these charges. Every effort should be made to get the L/C right the first time since these changes can be time-consuming and expensive.

To expedite the receipt of funds, wire transfers may be used. Exporters should consult with their international bankers about bank charges for such services.

(1) Process of Payment under L/C

① The Applicant and the Beneficiary negotiate terms and conditions of the L/C.
② The Applicant applies to the Issuing Bank to issue the L/C.
③ The Issuing Bank issues the L/C and forwards it to the Advising Bank.
④ The Confirming Bank confirms the L/C to the Advising Bank.
⑤ The Advising Bank checks the apparent authenticity of the L/C and advises the L/C to the Beneficiary.
⑥ The Beneficiary checks if the L/C complies with the commercial agreements and if all terms and conditions specified in the L/C can be satisfied and ships the goods.
⑦ The Beneficiary assembles the documents specified by the Issuing Bank in the L/C and checks the documents for discrepancies with the L/C and presents

them to the Nominated Bank(Advising Bank).

⑧ The Nominated Bank(Advising Bank) bears the documents against terms and conditions of the L/C and forwards them to the Confirming Bank.

⑨ The Confirming Bank checks if the documents comply with the L/C and makes payment immediately(if the L/C is available by sight) or on a certain date (if L/C is available by deferred payment).

⑩ The Issuing Bank reimburses the funds to the Confirming Bank immediately after the payment.

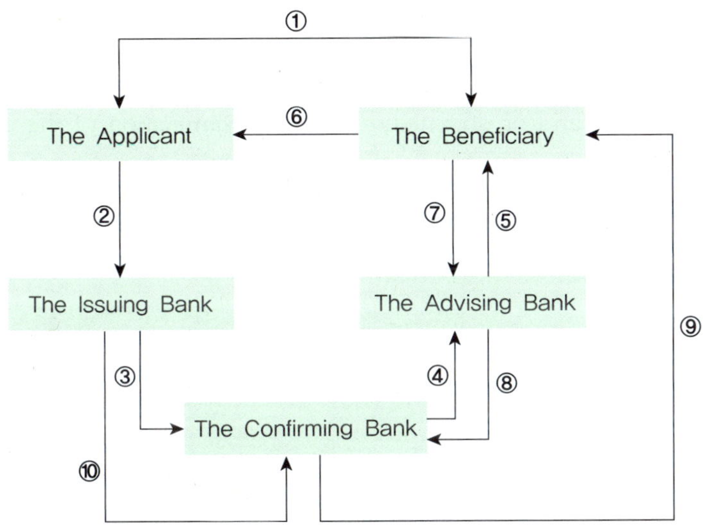

(2) Parties Involved in the L/C Procedure

① *Beneficiary*: Beneficiary means the party in whose favour a credit is issued.

② *Applicant*: Applicant means the party on whose request the credit is issued.

③ *The Advising Bank*: The Advising Bank advises you that an L/C has been received and available to you and informs you about the terms and conditions of the L/C. The advising bank is not responsible for the payment of the L/C.

④ *The Issuing Bank*: The Issuing Bank is the key player in the procedure, the one who makes the payment. Try to negotiate with the buyer which bank will issue the L/C. Ask the Advising Bank if it has a corresponding bank in the buyer's country and suggest this bank to the buyer as the issuing bank. If the Advising Bank does not have a corresponding bank in the buyer's country, ask the bank to recommend you a well-known bank with a high credit rating and insist your buyer has the L/C issued by this bank. The Advising Bank will be able to provide you with information on the financial status and credibility of the Issuing Bank.

⑤ *The Nominated Bank*: The Nominated Bank is the bank, which is authorised by the Issuing Bank "to pay, to incur a deferred payment undertaking, to accept Draft(s) or to negotiate." The Issuing Bank may authorise the Nominated Bank to negotiate the drafts and/or documents. Negotiation means that the nominated Bank – in this case the Negotiating Bank - gives value to such draft(s) and/or documents, not just examination of the documents.

⑥ *Confirming Bank*: Confirming Bank means the bank that adds its confirmation to a credit upon the issuing bank's authorization or request.

10-3 Financial Documents

In a GBT, quite a number of financial documents are used to ensure that the exporter receives full and timely payment for the shipment. These documents are usually issued by banks or exporters as follows.

- Application Form for International Money Transfer
- Drafts(Bills of Exchange)
- Banker's Drafts
- Commercial Drafts
- Sight Drafts
- Clean Drafts
- Documentary Drafts
- Application for Documentary Letter of Credit

• Letter of Credit

1. Application Form for International Money Transfer

When cash in advance or open account is used, payment may be effected by transferring money through banks. Thus, the overseas buyers need to complete the relevant application form for International Money Transfer. This kind of form is essentially a request to a bank to make an international money transfer on the remitter's behalf. In other words, an overseas buyer instructs a bank in the buyer's country to transfer an amount of money to an exporter's bank by M/T(Mail Transfer), T/T(Telegraphic Transfer) or D/D(Demand Draft).

2. Drafts(Bills of Exchange)

A draft or bill of exchange is an unconditional order signed by one party (the drawer) requesting a second party(drawee or payor) to make payment in lawful money immediately or at a determinable future time to a third party(payee). In the context of the GBT, the drawer and the payee is usually the seller while the drawee and payor is always the buyer. There are a banker's draft, commercial draft, sight draft, time draft, clean draft, documentary draft, etc., however, these drafts are not mutually exclusive, i.e. one draft can be a commercial, documentary, and time draft at the same time.

① *Banker's Draft*: A banker's draft is drawn by one bank on another bank. It is used in settling payment obligations between banks.

② *Commercial Draft*: A commercial draft is drawn by a firm or an exporter. The drawee can be a firm, an exporter or a bank. A commercial draft is commonly used in international trade in the settlement of payments.

③ *Sight Draft:* A sight draft is one that is payable in a specified number of days after 1) the date of issue; 2) the date of acceptance; 3) the date of B/L or a fixed future date. The specified number of days is called the "usance period."

[Figure 10-3] Process of Drawing a Bill of Exchange

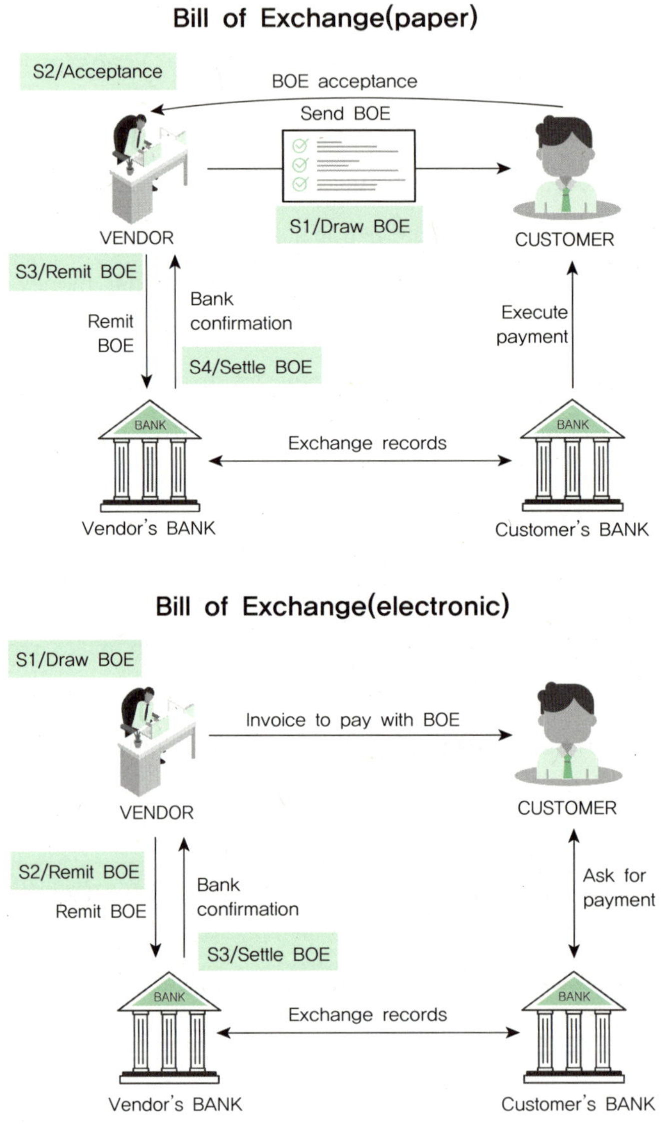

④ *Clean Draft*: A clean draft is one that is paid without the presentation of any other documents attached. A banker's draft is usually clean.

⑤ *Documentary Draft:* A documentary draft is one that should be paid only when certain documents have been attached to and presented together with the draft. Commercial drafts are usually documentary. The most important document is the bill of lading(B/L) that represents the title to the goods.

In the collection method of the payment of goods, a draft is always drawn upon the importer by the exporter to get paid. The exporter through the banking system, gets payment against the delivery just by a draft, for the sum agreed as settlement in the export contract. By using a draft with other shipping documents through the banking system, an exporter can ensure greater control of goods, because until the draft is paid or accepted by the overseas buyer, the goods cannot be released.

[Model Letter 10-1: Drafts(Bills of Exchange)]

Bill of Exchange

London, 27 Sept 1999 **Amount** £ 25,000.00

At 60 Days after Sight **pay against this Sole Bill of Exchange**

to the order of Ourselves

the sum of Twenty five thousand Pounds Sterling

for value Received

To:

International Buyers Limited
35th Floor, Two Exchange Square
Connaught Place
Hong Kong

For and on behalf of

UK Exporters Limited

J Jones

J Jones
Managing Director

3. Application for Documentary Letter of Credit

An application for a documentary letter of credit is the form used by the buyer to request his/her bank to open a documentary letter of credit in favour of the seller. It is used to authorise a bank to open a letter of credit.

4. Letter of Credit(L/C)

As one of the most important finance documents used in international trade, accuracy in the content of an L/C is of vital importance. Usually, an exporter will be advised of the issuing of an L/C well before the shipment, so that he/she could have enough time to check the details contained in it.

[Figure 10-4] Process of Issuing a Letter of Credit(L/C)

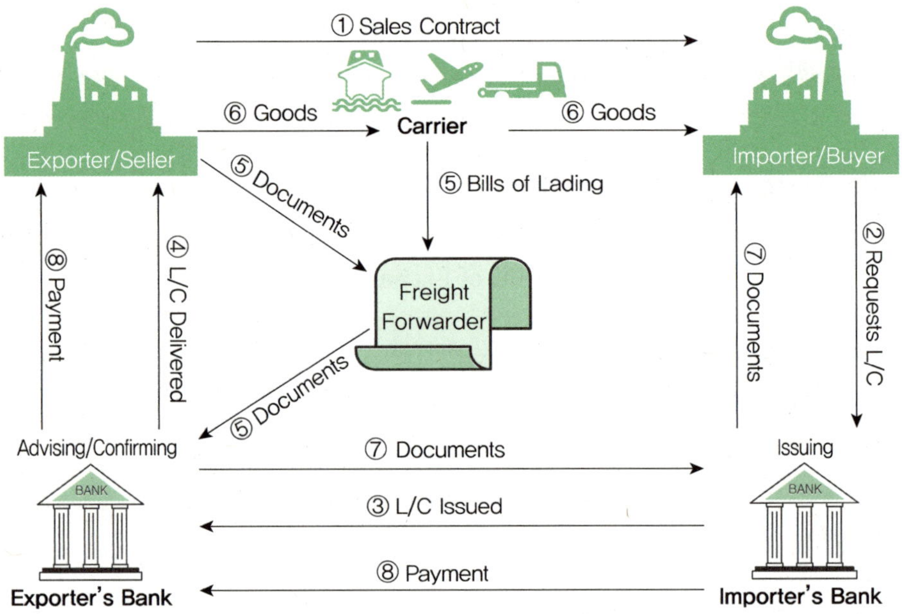

[Model Letter 10-2: SWIFT MT 700 – Letter of Credit(L/C)]

Application header block :	
: Input/Output Identifer	: I Outgoing Message
: Transaction Typer	: 700 issue of a documentary credit
: Transaction Prioity	: n Normal
: From	: WOORI BANK, SEOUL
: To	: HANKOOK BANK HONG KONG BRANCH, HONG KONG

Text Block :	
/27 : sequence of total	: 1/1
/40A : form of documentary credit	: IRREVOCABLE
/20 : documentary credit number	: M1234 606NS00018
/31C : date of issue	: 06/06/20
/31D : date and place of expiry	: 06/08/20 HONG KONG
/50 : applicant	: KOREA TOYS CO., LTD. 159-1SAMSUNGDONG KANGNAMGU, SEOUL, KOREA
/59 : beneficiary	: CHINA TOYS CO., LTD. RM 1000 CHAI WAN IND. CITY PHASE 1, 60 WING TAIRO, CHAIWAN H.K.
/32B : currency code amount	: USD 119,000.00
/39A : pct credit amount toterance	: 10/10
/41D : available with by name, address	: ANY BANK BY NEGOTIATION
/42C : drafts at	: AT SIGHT
/42A : drawee	: HONG KONG FIRST BANK LTD., HONG KONG(ADDR 2007, JARDINE HOUSE 1 CONNAUGHT PLACE, CENTRAL, HONG KONG)
/43P : partial shipment	: ALLOWED
/43T : transshipment	: NOT ALLOWED
/44A : on board/Disp/taking charge	: SHIDAO, CHINA
/44B : for transportion to	: BUSAN, KOREA
/44C : latest date of shipment	: 06/08/20

/45A : descr goods and/or services

700PAIRS OF CHINESE GIANT BEAR TOY
SIZE : MIN 1.5 METERS AT USD170.00
F.O.B.SHIDAO.CHINA

/46A : documents required

+SIGNED COMMERCIAL INVOICE IN QUINTUPLICATE
+PACKING LIST IN TRIPLICATE
+FULL SET OF CLEAN ON BOARD OCEAN BILL OF LANDING MADE OUT TO THE ORDER OF WOORI BANK MARKED FREIGHT COLLECT AND NOTIFY APPLICANT
+CERTIFICATE OF ORIGIN

/47A : additional conditions

ALL DOCUMENTS MUST BEAR OUR CREDIT NUMBER M1234 606NS00018
T/T REIMBURSEMENT NOT ALLOWED
OUANTITY 10PCT MORE OR LESS ALLOWED
+THIRD PARTY DOCUMENTS ACCEPTABLE

/71B : charges	: ALL BANKING COMMISSIONS AND CHARGES INCLUDING REIMBURSEMENT CHARGES OUTSIDE KOREA ARE FOR ACCOUNT OF BENEFICIARY
/49 : confirmation instructions	: WITHOUT
/53A : reimbursement bank	: HONG KONG FIRST BANK LTD., HONG KONG(ADDR 2007, JARDINE HOUSE 1 CONNAUGHT PLACE, CENTRAL, HONG KONG)

/78 : instructions to the pay/acc/neg bk

DRAFTS MUST BE SENT TO DRAWEE BANK FOR YOUR REMBURSEMENT
AND ALL DOCUMENTS TO US BY COURIER SERVICE IN ONE LOT

/72 : sender to receiver information	: THIS CREDIT IS SUBJECT TO U.C.P(1993 REVISION) I.C.C. PUBLICATION NO. 600

10-4 Model Letter of Payment(based on L/C)

1. Urging the Issuing of L/C

In the following cases, it is necessary for the seller to urge the buyer to issue the L/C.

① The buyer failed to issue an L/C within the time stipulated in the contract. In this case, the buyer breached the contract. However, if the seller still does not want to break off the transaction, he/she may urge the buyer to issue the L/C. The seller, though, reserves the right to claim against the buyer.

② In case the seller has already got the goods ready and is prepared to advance shipment, he/she may inquire of the buyer whether advanced shipment is allowed.

2. Examining L/C

After receiving the L/C, the exporter must examine the L/C against the sales contract. The examination should be covered with the following points.

① *The Political Background and Financial Standing of the Issuing Bank*: If the issuing bank is domiciled in a country which has friendly relations with Korea, but its nationality is not acceptable, this credit is not acceptable. If the issuing bank is a very small bank with a very poor financial standing, this credit is unacceptable too.

② *The Nature of the Credit and the Liabilities of the Issuing Bank*: Credit with a word like "revocable" is not acceptable. The undertaking clause of the issuing bank should be included. Sometimes there is the word "irrevocable" in the L/C, some "limitation clauses" regarding the undertaking of the issuing bank also include such clauses as "This credit is not effective until we receive the notification of import licenses."

* The above two points are also the examining focuses of the notifying bank.

③ *The Amount and Currency*: The amount and currency in the credit should conform to the contract. If there is a more or less clause in the contract, the amount of the L/C should cover the more or less part. The unit price and the total price should be correct.

④ *The Quality, the Quantity, Packing Clauses*

⑤ *The Date of Shipment, the Date and Place of Validity*: There is usually a reasonable interval between the date of shipment and the date of validity. In this way, the seller has sufficient time to prepare documents and make settlement.

⑥ *The Documents*: The types and scopes of documents are required as well as the methods of filling them out.

⑦ *Other Special Clauses*: Other special clauses are also required to designate the shipping company, the nationality, age and class of the ship, etc.

3. Amendment to L/C

Upon receipt of a letter of credit(L/C), the beneficiary finds that the terms stipulated in the credit are not in line with those mentioned in the contract; he/she must immediately notify the applicant in the shortest possible time. But he/she should also bear in mind that before receipt of the advice of the L/C amendment from the issuing bank, he/she should not start to make shipment, otherwise he/she is liable to some very unfavourable situations.

To remind, examine and amend the L/C. In practice, the L/C is jointly examined by both the bank that will lay the emphasis on the examination of the political backgrounds, credit standing and payment obligations and the exporting company who will focus on the examination of the conformity of the L/C content within the contract.

[Model Letter 10-3: Reminder for expected L/C opening]

To whom it may concern:

We invite your attention to the fact that the letter of credit covering your order No.121 has not reached us in spite of our repeated requests.

We urged our suppliers to execute an early delivery of products at higher prices to suit your requirements, which we trust you will meet with approval.

As we have not received your L/C we may be forced to cancel your order. However, we would prefer you to establish your L/C by the end of August so that we can continue our usual friendly business relations.

Yours faithfully,

[Model Letter 10-4: Notice of issuance of letter of credit]

Dear Sirs,

We are pleased to inform you that we have instructed our bank, The Hana Bank, Kangnam Branch, Seoul to open an irrevocable Letter of Credit for US$300,000 valid until August 31, in your favor. This credit will be confirmed by our banker's correspondences. The Citi Bank, which will let you have it within several days by registered mail.

We would request you to attach the following documents, viz full sets of bill of lading, three commercial invoices, one insurance policy, three packing lists, certificate & list of weight and/or measurement to your sight draft when negotiating it through your bankers.

The price you quoted us being CIF Busan, the amount of our credit will cover the amount of your invoice and also the cost of freight and insurance.

We hope that you will execute our order for six hundred units of your computer model, DB400S7B i3-7 to our complete satisfaction as usual.

Yours truly,

[Model Letter 10-5: Notice of issuance of letter of credit]

Dear Mr. Kim:

Thank you for your letter of July 14 containing your firm off for 800 dozen bottles of Red wine. We are pleased to accept your offer and would like to place order with you. We have enclosed our order form No. A-235.

We have instructed our bank, The Busan bank, to open an irrevocable letter of credit in your favor for US$555,500.00. The letter of credit will be valid until Dec.15, 2023. The letter of credit will be sent to you through our advisory bank, The National Australian bank. The letter of credit will cover your invoice for the amount of the merchandise CIF Busan.

Please attach the following documents to your sight draft when you present it for negotiation at the bank.

B/L (full sets)
Commercial invoices (3 copies)
Insurance policy
Packing list (2 copies)

We look forward to receiving confirmation when shipment has been made.

Sincerely yours,

[Model Letter 10-6: Notice of receipt of letter of credit]

Dear Sirs,

We have just been informed by the Hong Kong and Shanghai Banking Corporation, Seoul, that they received through their Head Office your L/C No. PS-701 of your order No.123.

We are going to ship the goods by M/V "Sun Star" sailing from Busan on the 21th of this month, As soon as we finish shipping your order, we will let you know the estimated time of arrival.

Thabk you for your prompt arrangement of the L/C.

Sincerely yours,

[Model Letter 10-7: Asking for amendment of L/C]

To whom it may concern:

We thank you for the irrevocable letter of credit No. 2130 of August 1 covering the contract of steel plates.

However, the stipulation given in the credit on the port of shipment is putting us in trouble in the execution of the order, because there is a discrepancy between our contract and the L/C.

Please amend it by cable as follows:
The words, "from Inchon" are to be replaced by "from Busan."

We have already booked a space on M.S. "Silverstar" sailing on September 20. If the letter of amendment reaches us by the end of this month, the shipment will be made in time.

Your prompt attention on this matter will ensure satisfactory delivery

Yours faithfully,

Key Expressions & Technical Terms

✔ **Accepting Bank**: Bank which accepts a bill of exchange by countersigning (endorsing) it, and thus incurs the legal obligation of paying the bill's amount on its maturity date. See also advising bank.

✔ **Advising Bank**: An advising bank(also known as a notifying bank) advises a beneficiary(exporter) that a letter of credit(L/C) opened by an issuing bank for an applicant(importer) is available. Advising Bank's responsibility is to authenticate the letter of credit issued by the issuer to avoid fraud. The advising bank is not necessarily responsible for the payment of the credit which it advises the beneficiary of. The advising bank is usually located in the beneficiary's country. It can be (1) a branch office of the issuing bank or a correspondent bank, or (2) a bank appointed by the beneficiary. Important point is the beneficiary has to be comfortable with the advising bank.

✔ **Bills of Exchange(Drafts)**:

1. defines a bill of exchange as: 'an unconditional order in writing, addressed by one person to another, signed by the person giving it, requiring the person to whom it is addressed to pay on demand, or at a fixed or determinable future time, a sum certain in money to or to the order of a specified person, or to bearer.'
2. defines a cheque as: 'a bill of exchange drawn on(behalf of) a banker, which is payable on demand(by banker).'
3. defines a promissory note as: 'an unconditional promise in writing made by one person to another, signed by the maker, engaging to pay on demand, or at a fixed or determinable future time, a sum certain in money to or to the order of a specified person or to bearer.'

✔ **Cash before Delivery**: a method of doing business in which a company will only send goods to a customer after they have received the customer's payment: If the company in question has poor references from suppliers, request cash before delivery.

✔ **Cash in Advance**: When an importer must pay the exporter in cash before a shipment is made. The logic behind the structure of such a transaction is that if an exporter ships a product to an importer and the importer does not pay for the item, the exporter has very little recourse. This term can be used in a variety of businesses, but it is most common in the import/export business.

✔ **Confirmed L/C**: A second guarantee, in addition to a letter of credit, that commits to payment of the letter of credit. A confirmed letter of credit is typically used when the issuing bank of the letter of credit may have questionable creditworthiness and the seller seeks to get a second guarantee to assure payment.

✔ **Confirming Bank**: Bank in an exporter's country which guarantees that the letter of credit established by the importer(for the benefit of the exporter) will be honored once the conditions therein are fully complied with. The confirming bank(Also called the advising bank) undertakes this responsibility on an arrangement(called confirmation) with the importer's bank which issued the letter of credit(called the issuing bank).

✔ **D/A(Documents against Acceptance)**: An arrangement in which an exporter instructs a bank to hand over shipping and title documents(see document of title) to an importer only if the importer accepts the accompanying bill of exchange or draft by signing it.

✔ **D/D(Demand Draft)**: A demand draft is a negotiable instrument similar to a bill of exchange. A bank issues a demand draft to a client(drawer), directing another bank(drawee) or one of its own branches to pay a certain sum to the specified party(payee).

✔ **Deferred Payment**: A loan arrangement in which the borrower is allowed to start making payments at some specified time in the future. Deferred payment arrangements are often used in retail settings where a person buys and receives and item with a commitment to begin making payments at a future date.

✔ **Documentary Letter of Credit(LC)**: LC is a written undertaking given by a bank on behalf of an Importer to pay the Exporter a given sum of money within a specified time, providing that the Exporter presents documents which comply with the terms laid down in the Letter of Credit. Letters of Credit can be for any amount, in any freely traded currency, and, subject to the presentation of compliant documents, may be payable: at sight, which means as soon as a compliant set of documents are presented to the paying bank; or, after a specified term, e.g. at 30, 60, 90 or 180 days of sight or Bill of Lading date. If the documents are not presented exactly as specified in the Letter of Credit, payment will not be made unless the Importer gives their authority to waive or amend the specified condition. A fundamental principle of Letters of Credit is that banks deal with documents and not with the goods to which the documents refer.

✔ **Document of Title**: Formal commercial document(such as bill of sale, certificate of title, title deed) or shipping document(such as a bill of lading, dock receipt, warehouse receipt) that confers and/or proves ownership. A document of title enables its holder(possessor) to receive, retain, sell, or otherwise dispose of the document and the goods or property listed therein.

✔ D/P(Documents against Payment): An arrangement under which an exporter instructs the presenting bank to hand over shipping and title documents(see document of title) to the importer only if the importer fully pays the accompanying bill of exchange or draft. Also called cash against documents.

✔ Drawee: A legal and banking term used to describe the party that has been directed by the depositor to pay a certain sum of money to the person presenting the check or draft. A typical example is if you are cashing a paycheck. The bank that cashes your check is the drawee, your employer who wrote the check is the drawer, and you are the payee.

✔ Irrevocable L/C: Irrevocable Letter Of Credit(ILOC) is a letter of credit type which can not be cancelled or amended by the issuing bank without the agreement of the parties of the letter of credit transaction. For example, issuing bank has no power to modify letter of credit terms if beneficiary does not find them acceptable. In other words, every amendment at least requires beneficiary's acceptance in order to be effective. Irrevocable letters of credit give much more payment security to the beneficiaries than revocable letters of credit because of the reasons explained above. As a result irrevocable letters of credit are the types of LCs that dominantly seen on the market place.

✔ L/C Amendment: An amendment is a formal or official change made to a law, contract, constitution, or other legal document. It is based on the verb to amend, which means to change. Amendments can add, remove, or update parts of these agreements. They are often used when it is better to change the document than to write a new one.

✔ **Negotiating Bank**: In a letter of credit transaction, the bank that:

- receives and examines the seller's documents for adherence to the terms and conditions of the letter of credit,
- gives value to the seller, so long as the terms of the credit have been met, and
- forwards them to the issuing bank(the buyer's or importer bank).

Depending upon the of credit, the negotiating bank will either credit or pay the seller/exporter immediately under the terms of the letter of credit, or credit or pay the exporter once it has received payment from the issuing bank. See advising bank; issuing bank.

✔ **Nominated Bank**: Nominated Bank — the bank with which credit is available. If no bank is mentioned in the credit as nominated bank, all banks are "nominated."

✔ **Promissory Note**: A promissory note is a legal instrument(more particularly, a financial instrument), in which one party(the maker or issuer) promises in writing to pay a determinate sum of money to the other(the payee), either at a fixed or determinable future time or on demand of the payee, under specific terms. If the promissory note is unconditional and readily salable, it is called a negotiable insrument.

✔ **Revocable L/C**: Revocable letter of credit can be modified or cancelled by the issuing bank after its issuance at any moment without seeking the beneficiary's consent. There is one exception regarding the revocation of the credit. Issuing bank must reimburse any nominated or confirming bank with which the recovable letter of credit has been made available if these banks fulfil their obligations under the documentary credit terms against complying presentation before they receive the amendment or cancellation notice from the issuing bank.

✔ **Sight Draft/Time Draft**: A banker's acceptance, or BA, is a promised future payment, or time draft, which is accepted and guaranteed by a bank and drawn on a deposit at the bank. The banker's acceptance specifies the amount of money, the date, and the person to which the payment is due. After acceptance, the draft becomes an unconditional liability of the bank. But the holder of the draft can sell(exchange) it for cash at a discount to a buyer who is willing to wait until the maturity date for the funds in the deposit.

✔ **SWIFT**: The Society for Worldwide Interbank Financial Telecommunication (SWIFT) provides a network that enables financial institutions worldwide to send and receive information about financial transactions in a secure, standardized and reliable environment. SWIFT also sells software and services to financial institutions, much of it for use on the SWIFTNet Network, and ISO 9362. Business Identifier Codes(BICs, previously Bank Identifier Codes) are popularly known as "SWIFT codes".

✔ **T/T(Telegraphic Transfer)**: Telegraphic Transfer or Telex Transfer, often abbreviated to T/T, is a historic term used to refer to an electronic means of transferring funds abroad. A transfer charge is often charged by the sending bank and in some cases by the receiving bank.

Check-up Questions 10

Q1 After receiving the Letter of Credit(L/C), the exporter must examine the L/C against the sales contract. Which one is NOT a concern while checking the L/C?

① The political background and financial standing of the issuing bank
② The nature of the credit and the liabilities of the negotiating bank
③ The quality, the quantity, packing clauses
④ The date of shipment, the date and place of validity

Q2 Write the following sentence in English.

귀사가 요구한 대로 당사는 7월 말까지 건설용 중장비 CHE-4003의 선적을 CKD 상태로 준비하고 있습니다. 8월 말까지 유효한 취소불능 신용장을 당사를 수익자로 하여 발행하여 줄 것을 요청드립니다.

[Useful expressions]
- As requested: 요구한 대로
- Heavy Construction Equipment: 건설용 중장비
- in our favour: 당사를 수익자로 하여
- to issue: 발행하다

➡

Q3 Write the following sentence in English.

강관 SP-5051에 대한 주문을 1회에 전부 선적할 수 없다는 귀사의 통지를 막 받았습니다. 당사는 거래은행에 분할선적을 허용하도록 신용장 조건의 수정을 지시했습니다.

[Useful expressions]

- Steel Pipe product SP-5051: 강관 SP-5051
- to ship at one time: 1회에 전부 선적하다
- partial shipment: 분할선적
- to allow(permit): 허락하다
- the terms of L/C: 신용장의 조건
- to amend(adjust): 수정하다

➥

Q4 Explain the following words and make a document.

① Bill of Exchange

② Documentary Letter of Credit(LC)

③ Document of Title

④ D/P(Documents against Payment)

⑤ T/T(Telegraphic Transfer)

11

CHAPTER

Global Business English

Follow-up Phase

Chapter

11 Follow-up Phase

Key Sentences

At the Follow-up Phase, claims by trading partners involved may occur and the dispute settlement procedure between the contracting parties will be determined.

Objectives

After studying this lesson, you will be able to:

- understand the definition of claim
- identify Management of Claims and Disputes

국제 비즈니스는 다른 비즈니스, 고객, 공급업체 및 거래 파트너 간에 정기적으로 잠재적 충돌에 직면한다. 협상을 통해 많은 문제를 신속하고 효과적으로 처리할 수 있지만 해결되지 않은 일부 분쟁은 비즈니스의 수익성과 생산성에 영향을 미칠 수 있다. 관련 거래 당사자의 클레임이 발생할 수 있으며 계약당사자 간의 분쟁 해결 절차는 이 단계에서 결정된다.

International businesses face regular potential conflicts between other businesses, customers, suppliers and trading partners. Many can be dealt with quickly and effectively through negotiation, yet some disputes that remain unresolved may affect the profitability and productivity of a business.

Alternative dispute resolution, for example, is the practice of settling such disputes without using conventional legal modalities(e.g. the court proceedings). There are three commonly used methods of resolving disputes without going to court: negotiation, mediation, arbitration.

11-1 Claims between Businesses

These are claims or disputes over terms of trade with suppliers, predatory pricing, misuse of market positioning, misleading or deceptive conduct, and can involve suppliers, operators in both his/her own country or other nations around the world, and competitors.

Sales contracts can suffer from breaches in performance and disputes are commonly focused on price, delivery of goods, quality and customer service standards.

Claims regarding the Trade Practices cases involve areas such as price fixing, price discrimination, restraint of trade(including certain types of exclusive dealings), abuse of market power(i.e. called Market Claim), misleading/deceptive conduct and unconscionable conduct(i.e. referring to Intentional Claim).

11-2 Management of Claims and Disputes

The goals of claims and dispute resolution are firstly to establish the right of any party to submit a claim, and secondly to enable the other party to consider the claim in terms of its validity, contractual terms and possible outcome.

1. The methods used to resolve disputes

The methods used to resolve disputes include the litigation(traditional route) and alternative dispute resolution(ADR) processes such as negotiation, mediation, conciliation, and arbitration.

The following diagram(please refer to Figure 11-1) illustrates the difference between litigation and all ADR processes.

[Figure 11-1] Difference between Litigation and All ADR Processes

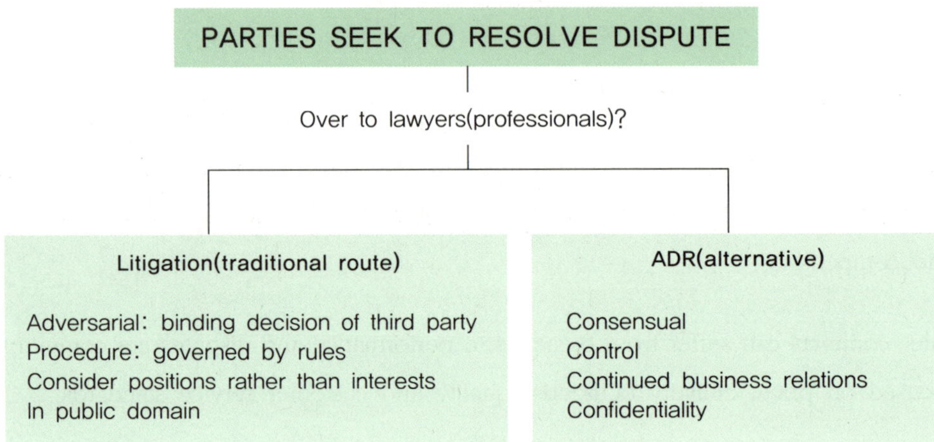

(1) Negotiation

In negotiation, both parties attempt to reach an agreement or settlement of disputes through give and take in an informal discussion. Third parties are not involved in negotiations.

(2) Mediation

Mediation is a dynamic, structured, interactive process where a neutral third party assists disputing parties in resolving conflict through the use of specialized communication and negotiation techniques. All participants in mediation are encouraged to actively participate in the process. Mediation is a "party-centered" process in that it is focused primarily upon the needs, rights, and interests of the parties. The mediator uses a wide variety of techniques to guide the process in a constructive direction and to help the parties find their optimal solution. In mediation, a neutral third party assists the negotiations but does not render a binding decision. A disinterested third party acts as a go-between to help resolve disputes among parties themselves.

(3) Conciliation

Conciliation is an alternative dispute resolution(ADR) process whereby the parties to a dispute use a conciliator, who meets with the parties both separately and together in an attempt to resolve their differences. They do this by lowering tensions, improving communications, interpreting issues, encouraging parties to explore potential solutions and assisting parties in finding a mutually acceptable outcome. Conciliation differs from mediation in that in conciliation, often the parties are in need of restoring or repairing a relationship, either personal or business.

(4) Arbitration

In some countries, arbitration is a process provided by an act of law, adopted by parties through mutual agreement stipulating that they will submit any dispute that may arise between them to the impartial judgement of some third party of their choice and that the award by this impartial person will be final and binding. Arbitration is not a new process; in fact, it was known to the Romans, used by the Dutch and English in the days of colonial expansion and is currently widely used in the global business transactions and further afield.

Arbitration is a more formal process than the dispute-resolution processes mentioned earlier, but arbitration has many advantages.

(5) Litigation

In litigation, an accusing party(the plaintiff) files a lawsuit against an accused party (the defendant) with a judicial court of a country. The court system renders a judgment or a decision based on relevant law and the facts. Litigation is the most expensive and time-consuming method of dispute settlement. In many cases, it takes several years to get a court date. Parties must do their best to resolve disputes through means other than litigation not only to save time and money, but also to avoid bad publicity.

Figure 11–2 on the following page shows the various dispute-resolution methods and purposes, as well as the position of each.

[Figure 11–2] Claims: Various Types of Dispute Resolution

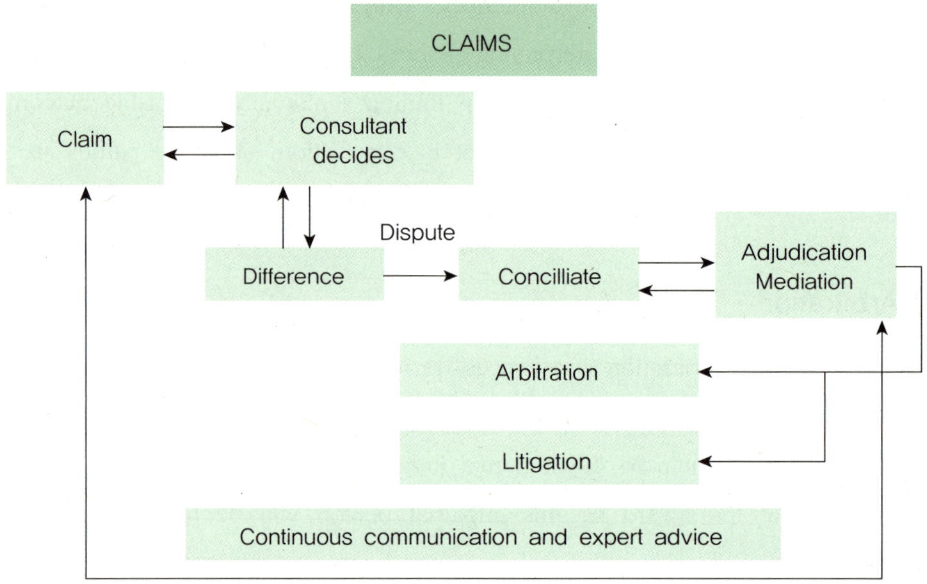

2. Sample Letters of Claims

[Model Letter 11–1: Claim on inferior quality]

To whom it may concern:

We received today the Nylon Goods which we ordered on December 2, 2022, but with great regret we have to inform you that their quality is inferior to the sample on which we passed you the order.

By separate mail we have sent you a cutting from this material, also one from the sample, so that you can compare the two. You will no doubt admit that your shipment does not come up to the sample supplied.

Yours truly,

[Model Letter 11-2: Claim on delay in delivery]

To whom it may concern:

Our Order No. MMK-102 for Christmas Illumination Sets
These goods reached here on December 15, six weeks after the stipulated date. As we have repeatedly advised you, this arrival date is too late for the season and the goods are therefore of little use to us.

Normally, under these circumstances, we would refuse to accept them. However, if a reasonable allowance of, say, 20%, can be made, we would be able to take them for the next season.

Please let us know by return whether this would be acceptable to you.

Very truly yours,

[Model Letter 11-3: Claim on damaged goods]

To whom it may concern:

This is to inform you that we have received 10 cases of Typewriters shipped by the S.S. "Penguin" of SK line per our order No.303, but found cases No.4 and No.8 badly damaged.

We are of the opinion that the cases were too fragile and the packing was not sufficient for export.

We enclose a survey report showing damage to be the result of faulty packing. We ask you therefore to send us a check for US $80.00 covering the loss we paid for the import duty and survey report including the charge for repair or to reship the new items at your expense. Upon arrival we will return the cargo with freight forward.

Your prompt attention of this matter is urgently requested.

Yours truly,

[Model Letter 11-4: Claim on delay in shipment]

To whom it may concern:

We wish to confirm your fax to the effect that you will airmail by American Air Line on December 10 your special Neckties regarding our Order No. 156.

Accordingly they were scheduled to arrive here about a week before Christmas, but unfortunately they reached us only yesterday: three weeks later than scheduled, and no fax followed explaining the reason for this delay.

We strongly stipulated, as you recall, that the goods be delivered here by December 20 at the latest, that is, we must have them well in advance for Christmas sales. As the shipment was delayed, the goods are now overstocked.

In view of these circumstances, we should like to propose that we accept the goods only if you reduce the price by 10%.

We hope to hear from you about the reason for this delay and also let us know if you will accept our proposal.

Very truly yours,

[Model Letter 11-5: Reply to claim about inferior goods]

To whom it may concern:

We have received your letter dated January 19 and thank you for sending us two samples of Nylon Goods for examination.

Tracing our records we find that a mistake was indeed made in packing by our shipping clerk misreading the item numbers.

In order to adjust the matter, we would like to give you a special allowance of 15% for this shipment.

Yours very truly,

[Model Letter 11-6: Reply to claim about delay in delivery]

To whom it may concern:

We have just received your letter dated December 17, and regret to learn about the late arrival of the shipment of your Order No. MMK-102. Since we have no idea what caused this delay, we have begun an immediate investigation of the matter with our shipping company.

We apologize for what has happened and in order to make adjustment we ask you to accept the goods at a reduction of 20%, as you proposed.

We thank you for calling our attention to this matter. Please accept our apologies for the trouble we have caused you.

We assure you that we shall take every care to prevent similar errors in the future.

Very truly yours,

[Model Letter 11-7: Reply to claim about damaged goods]

To whom it may concern:

Thank you for your letter dated August 22 concerning the 100 cases of Typewriters covering your order No.303.

After careful investigation, we could not find any error on our part because we made every effort to fulfil your order as evident from the certificate of packing inspection enclosed. Moreover the lots were shipped on board the ship in perfect condition which is clearly stated in the clean B/L.

We suggest, therefore, that you lodge a claim with the insurance company. We will assist you wherever possible to process the claim.

Though it was quite beyond our control, we are very sorry for the inconvenience you have suffered.

We assure you that we will make every attempt to prevent such a recurrence in the future.

Yours very truly,

Key Expressions & Technical Terms

✔ **Alternative Dispute Resolution(ADR)**: Alternative dispute resolution(ADR; known in some countries, such as Australia, as external dispute resolution) includes dispute resolution processes and techniques that act as a means for disagreeing parties to come to an agreement short of litigation. It is a collective term for the ways that parties can settle disputes, with(or without) the help of a third party

✔ **Arbitration**: Arbitration, a form of alternative dispute resolution(ADR), is a technique for the resolution of disputes outside the courts. The parties to a dispute refer it to arbitration by one or more persons(the "arbitrators", "arbiters" or "arbitral tribuna"), and agree to be bound by the arbitration decision(the "award"). A third party reviews the evidence in the case and imposes a decision that is legally binding on both sides and enforceable in the courts.

Arbitration is often used for the resolution of commercial disputes, particularly in the context of international commercial transactions. In certain countries such as the United States, arbitration is also frequently employed in consumer and employment matters, where arbitration may be mandated by the terms of employment or commercial contracts.

✔ **Conciliation**: Conciliation is willingness to end a disagreement or the process of ending a disagreement.

Conciliation is an alternative dispute resolution(ADR) process whereby the parties to a dispute use a conciliator, who meets with the parties both separately and together in an attempt to resolve their differences. They do this by lowering tensions, improving communications, interpreting issues, encouraging parties to explore potential solutions and assisting parties in finding a mutually acceptable outcome.

- Conciliation differs from arbitration in that the conciliation process, in and of itself, has no legal standing, and the conciliator usually has no authority to seek evidence or call witnesses, usually writes no decision, and makes no award.
- Conciliation differs from mediation in that in conciliation, often the parties are in need of restoring or repairing a relationship, either personal or business.

✔ **Litigation**: In litigation an accusing party(the plaintiff) files a lawsuit against an accused party (the defendant) with a judicial court of a country.

✔ **Mediation**: Mediation is the attempt to help parties in a disagreement to hear one another, to minimise the harm that can come from disagreement (e.g. hostility or 'demonising' of the other parties) to maximize any area of agreement, and to find a way of preventing the areas of disagreement from interfering with the process of seeking a compromise or mutually agreed outcome.

✔ **Negotiation**: both parties attempt to reach an agreement or settlement of disputes through give and take in an informal discussion.

✔ **Quantity Surveyor**: A quantity surveyor(QS) is a professional working within the construction industry concerned with construction costs and contracts. A quantity surveyor differs from a building estimator in that a quantity surveyor is a formally trained and accredited professional(Bachelor's degree or higher) in the estimating field.

Check-up Questions 11

Q1 Translate the paragraph below into Korean.

International businesses face regular potential conflicts between other businesses, customers, suppliers and trading partners. Many can be dealt with quickly and effectively through negotiation, yet some disputes that remain unresolved may affect the profitability and productivity of a business. Alternative dispute resolution, for example, is the practice of settling such disputes without using conventional court proceedings.

➥

Q2 Which one of the following is the most cost-effective and legally-binding dispute resolution method?

① Adjudication ② Arbitration
③ Litigation ④ Mediation

Q3 Write the following paragraph in English.

당사의 디지털 카메라 DC-3004에 대한 무역클레임 No. 2020의 타당성을 인정할 수 있도록 동봉한 견본을 조사해 주시기 바라며, 또 어떤 해결방안을 준비하고 있는지 팩스나 이메일로 통지해 주십시오.

[Useful expressions]

- to admit the reasonableness(validity/justification): ~을 칭하다
- the enclosed sample: 동봉한 견본
- settlement(solution): 해결방안

➥

12 CHAPTER

Global Business English

English Resume

Chapter

12 English Resume

Key Sentences

A resume provides a summary of your education, work history, credentials, and other accomplishments and skills. There are also optional sections, including a resume objective and a career summary statement.

Objectives

After studying this lesson, you will be able to:

- understand the definition and tyoes of resume
- make three main types of resume

12-1 Concepts and Examples of English Resume

영문 이력서란

이력서는 어떤 직책에 채용되는 것을 목적으로 쓰는 자기소개서이다. 지원자가 제출한 사실에 기반한 정보를 기초로 서류의 심사자가 인터뷰 진행 여부를 결정하므로 심사자의 관심을 끌도록 강한 메시지를 포함해서 작성해야 한다. 영어로는 Resume 또는 CV(Curriculum Vitae)라고 하며, 지원자가 희망하는 직책을 찾아가는 것이 아니라, 고용자가 자신을 선택할 수 있도록 'We-attitude'가 아닌 'You-attitude'의 자세로 일반적으로 들어가야 하는 내용과 형식을 따르는 것이 좋다. 영문 이력서의 표준 양식은 크게 연대순 이력서, 기능적 이력서, 혼합형 이력서의 세 가지가 있다.

1. What Is a Resume?*

A resume provides a summary of your education, work history, credentials, and other accomplishments and skills. There are also optional sections, including a resume objective and a career summary statement.

A resume should be as concise as possible. Typically, a resume is one page long, although sometimes it can be as long as two or three pages.

Resumes come in a few types, including chronological, functional, and combination formats. Select a format that best fits the type of job you are applying for.

2. How to Write a Successful Resume

Choose the right format for your needs. Your industry, experience, and desired role will inform your choice of resume format — e.g., chronological, functional, or combination. See sample resumes, organized by occupation and industry.

Write for both robots and humans. Your resume needs to get past the applicant tracking system and grab the attention of the human being on the other end. These resume writing tips will help you craft a document that appeals to both software and the company's Human Resources department.

3. Examples of English Resume

The three main types of resume formats include.

① *Chronological resume*: For candidates with rich, consistent professional experience.

② *Functional resume*: For candidates with several gaps or changes in their career.

③ *Combination*: For candidates with a diverse background of experience or when skills and abilities are more relevant than work experience.

* https://www.thebalancemoney.com/cv-vs-resume-2058495#citation-1

(1) Chronological Resume

A chronological resume is a standard resume format that lists your work history in reverse chronological order, starting with your most recent job listed at the top and each previous position in descending order.

A chronological resume helps employers quickly understand the value of your most recent and relevant work experiences. As employers may only spend a few seconds on each resume, prioritizing the most recent information helps ensures your experience gets seen.

[Chronological Resume Example]

James Applicant
Edmond, OR
555-555-1212
james.applicant@email.com

OVERVIEW

Energetic and motivating leader with a proven ability to effectively manage both staff and long and short-term projects. A self-starter and strong independent worker who excels at analyzing products and procedures in order to generate new ideas that improve efficiency and production quality.

Background

Trade Show Intelligence
Marketing Plans
Market Research

PROFESSIONAL EXPERIENCE

COMFORT, INC., Edmond, OR
MANAGER (2018~Present)
Manage daily operations of a $1 million foam insulation company.

- Train and supervise work crews in more efficient product installation techniques resulting in reduced material waste by 20% and labor hours by 43%.
- Instrumental in developing sales team's knowledge in the areas of building science and energy conservation in order to provide customers with the information to successfully plan for, and utilize, spray foam insulation.

MILITARY BASE. Edmond, OR

DATA NETWORK MANAGER (2016~2018)

Managed command and control data network used to generate video representation of geographic area surrounding the ship. The team consisted of 38 individuals from four departments.

- Production Control Officer: Coordinated the efforts of 135 personnel utilizing 37,000 man hours. Completed 520 jobs totaling over $4 million during a 13-month refurbishment period.
- Assistant Command Duty Officer: Directed daily routine utilizing a duty section of 600 personnel from 12 different departments.

EDUCATION

UNIVERSITY of Texas Austin, TX

Master of Business Administration, 2021

Bachelor of Economics

(2) Functional Resume

A functional resume is a type of resume format which showcases skills over experience. The purpose of a functional resume is to draw attention to transferable abilities rather than focusing on a chronological overview of your work history.*

Should You Use One? In most cases, a functional resume is not the best option. There are two main reasons that many recruiters don't want to see functional resumes. It can be used to cover up significant career gaps and lack of relevant experience.

* ATS(Applicant Tracking System)이라고 불리는 자동 이력서 심사시스템

[Functional Resume Example]

John A. Doe
999 Main Street
Ann Arbor, MI 99999
(123) 555-1234
johndoe@email.com

CAREER OBJECTIVE

Experienced and versatile professional with strong urban planning as well as people, management, and research skills seeks a position in urban planning and environmental impact analysis with a major city or Fortune 500 company.

CORE QUALIFICATIONS

- Background managing direct transportation planning and programs
- Adept at managing urban planning programs and people
- Able to anticipate and project organizational change
- Background as administrator of office operations

EXPERIENCE AND SKILLS

- Skilled in Government Guidelines
- Quality Control
- Urban Planning
- Environmental Impact Mitigation and Research
- Urban Planning
- Geology/Hydrology
- Site Evaluations
- Computer Software Tools
- Scientific and Business Grant Writing

Administrative: Lead coordinator for the daily processing of thousands of checks for payment and the mailing of confidential reports, meeting strict deadlines, and avoiding late fees.

Problem Solving: Designed a waste-management program involving Recycle Ann Arbor and a major book company, intended for the efficient handling of tons of paper, cardboard, plastic, metal, and glass, achieving net savings of $20,000 per building annually and reducing company disposal obligations.

Management: Oversaw operations of an expanding research lab, providing expertise, commitment, and quality control during a time of significant transition.

EMPLOYMENT HISTORY

Senior Process Engineer, September 2018-Present
Zezee Corp., Ann Arbor, Mich.

Process Engineer: Technical Support, September 2014-September 2018
Zezee Corp., Ann Arbor, Mich.

Technical Professional, September 2012-September 2014
City of the Stars, Mich.

EDUCATION

Master of Business Administration (2017); GPA 3.9
Southern Nazarene University, Bethany, Okla. (Online Program)

Bachelor of Science (Emphasis: Ecosystem/Environmental Business) May 2014
Eastern Michigan University, Ypsilanti, Mich.

(3) Combination Resume

A combination resume lists your skills and qualifications first. Your employment history is listed next, in reverse chronological order(beginning with your current or most recent job and then working back through earlier positions).

This format often offers the best of both worlds for job seekers who might prefer to present their resume in a functional format, emphasizing their skills and qualifications, but who have been instructed by the employer to include a work history. For those who wish to avoid a traditional chronological resume — either because of unrelated jobs or employment gaps — this format is a good compromise.1

The combination resume is typically sectioned into two parts.

The first part is similar to a functional resume in that it highlights skills, achievements, and qualifications. The second part depicts the timeline of one's work experience.

[Combination Resume Example]

Joe Applicant

123 Main Street • Oakland, CA 12345 • (123) 456-7890 • joe.applicant@email.com

EDUCATION COORDINATOR/SUPERVISOR

Effectively managing staffs in both the blood bank and business arenas

Results-oriented, high-energy, hands-on professional with 10+ years' experience and a successful record of accomplishments in the blood banking, training, and communication transmission industries.

Key skills include

- Experience in Quality Assurance and Customer Service in Two Industries.
- Excellent Communication Skills
- Team Building & Leadership
- Internal & External Communications
- Experience in Training and Payroll

PROFESSIONAL EXPERIENCE

AMERICAN RED CROSS, Oakland, Calif.

EDUCATION MANAGER / EDUCATION COORDINATOR(February 2013 – Present)

Facilitated successful educational project over the past five years for Northern California blood centers, with FDA regulated manufacturing equipment, as pertaining to CGMP, CFRs, Calif. State and American Association of Blood Bank(AABB) regulations.

Notable accomplishments

- Provide daily operational review/quality control of educational accountability to meet regulations.
- Responsible for assuring uncompromised compliance with 23 organizational quality systems.

CORE COMMUNICATION INC., Sunnyvale, Calif.

CABLE TELEVISION SUPERVISOR(May 2008 - February 2013)

Supervised contract support for six AT&T Broadband systems located in the Bay Area.

Notable Accomplishments

- Provided customer support/resolution, training in telephony and customer care.
- Handled quality control, payroll, special projects/plant extensions, and staff evaluations.

EDUCATION & CREDENTIALS

SAN JOSE STATE UNIVERSITY, San Jose, Calif.

Bachelor of Science (GPA; 3.8; Major: Administration of Justice; Graduated Cum Laude), May 2008

Certifications

NCCT Phlebotomy Technician Certification • NCCT Certified • CATV System Technician

Information Technology Skills

Microsoft Office Suite • ADP/Workforce Now • Proficient in Various Payroll Software Systems

12-2 Concepts and Examples of Cover Letter

Cover Letter란

커버레터란 인사담당자 등에게 이력서(resume)와 함께 동봉하여 보내는 편지로 자기소개서의 축약본이라고 보면 된다. 인사담당자는 커버레터를 보고 지원자의 이력서를 읽을지를 판단한다. 외국계 기업에 지원할 경우 커버레터 없이 Resume만 보낼 경우 불합격의 요인이 될 수 있으므로 반드시 작성하는 것이 좋다.

이력서의 '표지' 격인 커버레터에는 어디에서 채용정보를 알았는지 보여주는 지원 경로, 지원 분야에 맞는 자격 요건, 간단한 프로필, 희망 연봉, 회사에 대한 관심도, 연락처 등을 한눈에 확인할 수 있도록 간략히 담아야 한다.

커버레터의 구성요소는 Header, Date, Inside Address, Subject, Salutation, Body, Closing, Writer's identification, Enclosure로 Business Letter와 유사하다.

1. What Is a Cover Letter?

A cover letter is an integral part of your job application, along with your resume. It's designed to introduce you in a more personal way, complementing the contents of the resume/CV, expanding on relevant skills and achievements, and highlighting a selection of your most prominent accomplishments.

2. What Is the Purpose of a Cover Letter?

A good cover letter persuades the employer your qualifications match their needs, plus.

- Shows you did research and take the job seriously.
- Proves you understand the challenges of the company.
- Reflects that your vision aligns with their goals.

• Presents how your skills and experience are a solution.

Ultimately, a good cover letter should be all about "why should we hire you" and "what's in it for us." The winning tactic here is focusing on them, not just on you, which will ultimately make you stand out from other applicants.

3. Examples of a Cover Letter

커버레터는 지원방식에 따라 크게 세 종류로 나눌 수 있다.

(1) Seeing a Ad and Applying

Dear Mr. Cruise

Your advertisement in the Korea Herald appealed to me for two reasons. You plan to open up a new branch of Seattle's Coffee; I seek the opportunity to manage a newly opened store. I am also interested in building my career in the coffee and tea industry. Therefore, I have decided to submit my resume in application for the position of Store Manager.

My relevant experience includes three years as an assistant store manager of Seattle's Coffee and my current position as store manager of Star Cafe. I look forward to discussing opportunities at Seattle's Coffee with you. I will call you next week to make sure you have received my resume and to set up a mutually agreeable time for us to seek.

Yours Sincerely,
Hilary Duff

Enc: Resume

(2) An Occasional Application

Dear Paris Hilton

I would like to express my interest in Ad Planning position of ACE Advertisement Company. After four years at Korea University, where I majored in English and wrote for the college paper. I leapt into the competitive world of advertising at Buy & Sell in Seoul. For the past year I have served a valuable apprenticeship in the advertising industry, working as an assistant account executive on the CJJ account. During my time on the CJJ account, the company's advertising spending has increased by two billion won, and I have progressed from having very little client contact to interesting with the client-side on a regular basis.

Since my introduction to the world of advertising, it has been my goal to work for Ace. I would like to discuss the position availability.

Thank you for your time spent reading this letter and the enclosed resume.
I look forward to hearing from you.

Sincerely,
Jerry Kim

(3) An Acquaintance's Recommendation

Dear Mr. B. Clinton

Jack Smith informed me that you might be looking for someone to fill the production assistant position for the movie you are filming. I worked with Jack last summer through an internship sponsored by the Miracle Corporation and found work to be very stimulating and well-suited to my talents. He suggested that an excellent first step in my career search would be a discussion with you.

I have enclosed my resume for your interview. I will try to contact you within the week to see if I can schedule an appointment with you.

Thank you for your consideration.

Yours truly,
Sun-ah Kim

12-3 Concepts and Examples of Self-introduction Letter

자기소개서란

자기소개서는 자기를 소개하는 글을 말한다. 대입 자기소개서, 취업 자기소개서 혹은 아르바이트를 시작하기 위해 이력서와 함께 필요한 사실상의 필수 문서이다.

보통 '자소서'로 줄여 부르는데, 내가 살아온 생애와 문제의식, 가치관, 삶의 태도 등을 어필함으로써 해당 회사 또는 대학에서 요구하는 인재상을 얼마나 충족시킬 수 있는가를 구체적으로 보여줄 수 있는 가장 좋은 무기 중 하나이다. 최근 들어 점점 그 중요성이 커지고 있다.

1. What is a Self-introduction Letter?

A Self introduction letter is something that you can use to introduce yourself to other people. This letter can be used in job applications, when writing your curriculum vitae and when you want to introduce yourself to others.

2. Advantages and Types of Self-introduction Letter

(1) Advantages of Self-introduction

A letter of introduction can forge a new connection. Use these letters to introduce yourself to a potential new client or employer, or to do the same for one of your contacts.

Keep your letter concise and to the point. The reader is a busy professional. State your purpose early on.

Consider sending your introduction via email. If time is of the essence, emailing your note can help make an introduction quickly.

Edit and proofread before sending. Even if you know the recipient well, make sure your letter is perfect before you mail or send it.

(2) Types of Self-introduction Letter

There are two types of letters of introduction.

In the first type, you introduce a connection to someone else you know. That someone might be a potential candidate for employment, or someone looking for career assistance.

In the other type of letter of introduction, you write to someone you haven't met. You introduce yourself to ask them for a job referral or request assistance with a job search.

3. Examples of Self-introduction Letter

[Sample 1]

Who I am

When I was 12 years old, I have studied Japanese. For me, it was very novel characters. I started studying for myself through watching drama and listening Japanese music. Time passed, because I was wondering about my Japanese level, so I found e-mail pen pal who are Japanese friends to check Japanese proficiency.

I felt pleasure to communicate with other people. So I was participated in student council of department for a year. When I was senior, I was in charge of Japanese part in Asia Academy. It consists of Korean and foreign students who live in Pusan. I feel worth to experience with foreign friends

Strength and Weakness

My strength is that I care about surrounding people. When I was a second year, I volunteered for foreigner who came to Pusan National University as exchange student. Some Japanese student also had a volunteer but she didn't support him well. So I helped him together. I helped Japanese students willingly when something happened. Then they called me oka-san that means mother in Japanese. I will say that my weakness is considering a long time. Even if it decided to act this time, I was considered about that. It is very important to consider carefully when I have to determine something for my job. But it is not good to me individually so I try to think more comfortable.

What I got from my life

I am highly interested in Japanese language. I have lived in Osaka, Japan for a year. I was exchange student in Osaka University. It had many events for foreign student to understand Japanese culture. I could find cultures that I didn't know in Korea. And I got a chance that foreign students went to middle or high school to introduce about own countries. It was very nice experience to me.

Besides, I found part time job and worked for a half year. Because I was a foreigner, it was difficult to find part time job. Fortunately, I worked at pancake café. All staff was Japanese except me so it was very hard. But from this experience, if I find my job in Japan, I can be quick to adapt.

Why I am interested in this job

I am interested in traveling, especially Japan area. When I lived in Osaka, it was short period but I went to some places. It was also recorded on my blog. And I think there are many hidden spots that it is not famous to Korean. I would like to introduce there and plan the trip schedule.

I am used to planning of Osaka, so it is rewarding that people reply it was good. Because I can speak Korean and Japanese, it is favorable for both people to plan travel packages.

[Sample 2]

Creativeness and original have been the most important part in my life. I have always pursued of being differentiated with anyone else, and tried my best to experience more in order to have my own distinctive individual personality. I believe that creativeness comes out if I experience many failures and have an opportunity to get back up again. Plus, I thought that choosing 'international trade' as my major in University will give me a wide range of learning experiences regarding Economics, Business, and law. In fact, I have been interested in Economics and Business because I believe that money have an significant power governing Capitalist society. In addition, I have also thought that in today's world, unfairness and injustices made by consequentialism acts and egoistic attitudes should be fixed. After getting an acceptance from my University, I have been trying my best to connect what I have learned from those three subjects and attempt the leadership experiences that I can do for the society. Even though I have introspective personality, I have joined in non-profit organisation runned by global youths that offers me to do some volunteer works, business practices and global experiences. Through 2 years of experiences while being in the organisation and also being a president of it, I have met so many people that needs us, many foreigners who applied to be one of our member of volunteering projects, CEOs of company that can invest money to us and students to join in the organisation. Since I need to manage hundreds of people and various teams and departments, I had to contemplate about how can I apply what I have been learning in University and the thing I should learn in addition to the subjects that I can learn from my major. With this experiences I have experienced many failures and had a tremendous opportunity to challenge. After all, I could develop my capability of having new ideas that differentiated from the traditions and the way how to think about stabilities of these ideas. Being logical and cool-headed attitude was learned from my challenges, failures and successes of Business and leadership fields. In the future, I hope I be someone who have a positive impacts to the world and keep the justice, law and order in the fields of business.

[Sample 3]

I am really honored to have a chance to submit my self-introduction to your company. I am planning to describe several reasons why you would want to recruit me as your new employee and hopefully these may appeal to your company.

My name is Seo-Kyung Lee, and I am 23 years old. I currently study at Pusan National University, which, I could proudly assure, is the best ranking university in Busan. It is scheduled that I graduate next year but I am trying to seek ways to finish school earlier than that. I major in English Education, in which most of the students share the same goal to become a teacher. Throughout my courses and various experiences, I mastered both in the field of English and Education respectively.

First of all, I am pretty confident of my English skills, and as the background, there lie two times of experiences abroad. I had stayed in England and America for one year each, when I was 9 years old and 15 years old. Nothing was easy especially when I went to England, because I had little understanding of the country's social customs as well as English itself. However, as I was getting along with my English friends, I became no more afraid of saying English out loud and spoke English even if there were many errors. Continuous hearing and reading English helped my ability to speak the language grow even more.

Years after I came back to Korea, I fortunately got another chance to live abroad, this time in America. This time, speaking English was much easier for me with all the background information that I had acquired either directly or indirectly. However, making friends was not as easy as the former experience, since unlike before, I was not the only Asian in school, and no one was largely interested in an ordinary Asian girl. So I stood up and went to initiate conversations with the students, which was almost impossible to do with the timid personality that I used to have. I believe that in the process of making new friends in a foreign country helped me become outgoing and extroverted also in Korea. Not only that, but also I accomplished many assignments that involved the process of writing and revising, and kept an English diary myself, and this helped my writing skills grow better. With the progressed skills, I actively worked as a member of English Newspaper club when I was in high school. I also got accepted to another college with English essay, and I think this can prove my writing skills. So I would say that the experiences abroad grew both my character and my English ability. I recently achieved the score of 980 in TOEIC and am familiar with business terminologies. In the globalized age, you might want to seek for an outgoing worker that can negotiate and communicate well and that has a high level of ability to deal with English written documents.

You could easily think that 'Education' is not necessarily related to the position you have advertised, but in teaching profession courses, I have learned not only how to impart to students the knowledge in the subject I am in charge of, but also how to deal with students, since theses courses have many similarities with psychology. By this, I mean that I know how to manage students of various characteristics. I am sure that in any position in any sector, the most important element is 'smooth relationships', dealing with students has a lot in common with dealing with grown-ups. With the skills that I have learned, I have the conviction that I may help your company progress more favorably.

12-4 Concepts and Examples of English Recommendations

영문 추천서란

추천서란 입시, 채용, 포상, 각종 모집 등에서 선발에 적합하다고 생각되는 적합한 대상자에 대해 해당 분야의 전문인이나 지식이 높은 추천인이 추천의 글을 작성한 문서이다.

추천서의 핵심은 대상자를 표현하는 데 있어서, 추천하는 사람이 "이렇게 훌륭하다"는 것을 어떻게 효과적이고 신뢰성 있게 작성하는지가 관건이라 할 수 있다. 일반적으로 추천서를 보면 미사여구와 추상적인 칭찬 내지는 자랑 일변도의 글이 많은데 이러한 추천서는 설득력을 얻기가 어렵기 때문에 좋은 추천서가 될 수 없다.

1. What is a Letter of Recommendation?

A letter of recommendation is a letter written on behalf of an applicant by someone who can vouch for that person's educational or professional performance. This letter is typically sent to an admissions officer or hiring manager considering a candidate for admission, employment, or a scholarship.

2. Contents and Templates of English Recommendation

Keep your letter of recommendation brief and to the point. The last thing anyone wants is a multi-page letter. The hiring manager or person receiving the letter will want to know who you are, how you know the applicant, and why you are recommending them.

Here are Three Letter of Recommendation Templates.*

* https://www.betterteam.com/letter-of-recommendation

(1) Basic Letter of Recommendation

[Today's Date]

Dear [Mr./Mrs./Ms./To Whom it May Concern],

I am writing to recommend [full name of the person you're recommending] for [what you're recommending them for].

I have known [person you're recommending] since [date] as [capacity in which you've known the person, i.e., "good friend," "coworker," etc.].

I have always known [person you're recommending] to be [qualities the person has, such as "honest," "loyal," "hardworking"].

Based on our experience together, I can confidently recommend [person you're recommending] for [what you're recommending them for].

Sincerely,

[Your Name + Signature]

(2) Personal or Character Letter of Recommendation

Dear [Mr./Mrs./Ms./To Whom it May Concern],

I am writing to recommend [full name of person you're recommending] for [what you're recommending them for].

I have known [person you're recommending] for [number of months or years] as a [friend, coach, neighbor, etc.].
From my experience, [person you're recommending] is [qualities the person has, such as "honest," "kind," "easy to work with," etc.].

One example of [his/her/their] character is when [he/she/they] was/were [something specific he/she/they did that showed character].

Based on our experience together, I can confidently recommend [person you're recommending] for [what you're recommending the person for].

Sincerely,

[Your Name + Signature]

(3) Academic Letter of Recommendation

[Today's Date]

Dear [Mr./Mrs./Ms./To Whom it May Concern],

I am writing to recommend [full name of student you're recommending] for [what you' re recommending them for].

I have known [Person you're recommending] for [number of semesters, months or years]. [He/She/They] has been a student in my [list classes of your student has taken] classes. We've also worked on [any other projects you've worked on together].

I have always known [person you're recommending] to be [qualities the student has, such as "a dedicated student," "hardworking"].

I was especially impressed with [his/her/their] work on [specific task or project performed] where [he/she/they] was/were able to [something specific he/she/they accomplished].

Based on our experience together, I can confidently recommend [student you're recommending] for [what you're recommending the student for].
Sincerely,

[Your Name + Signature]

3. Examples of English Recommendations

Muma College of Business
University of South Florida
4202 E Fowler Ave, Tampa, FL 33620,
United States of America

July 1st 2016

Letter of Ms. Yeonwoo Jeon

Dear Sirs and Madames:

I am a professor of Trade department in Pusan National University and also working as vice president of Economy and Trade Graduate School. I know Ms. Yeonwoo Jeon very well as I taught her at her university. As I remember, she was a very excellent student who completed the undergraduate courses only in 7 semesters while serving as managing editor of English newspaper at university at the same time. This shows how diligent, humble and sociable she was.

After all, she entered Korea International Trade Association for which most graduates related to trade and economics hope to work and as a graduate from Pusan National University, she made the university more renowned. In addition, she has become a model for the students at the school job fair.

This year KITA, Pusan National University and Busan Ilbo are preparing for holding big joint celebrations marking the 70th anniversary. In recognition of her excellent talent, she is taking care of this project and often visiting the university for work. KITA also deals with the development of high skilled manpower in trade through education and training programs and she is said to take over the duties with the education programs in the future. She will do her best to grow local talents as well as working as a talented individual herself. The MIM of USF will be necessary for her to succeed in promoting talent development programs for the next few years.

One of the biggest problems that local offices have encountered is a brain drain to Seoul metropolitan area. Nonetheless, she's come back to Busan and tried to help local companies hoping for training more local talents. She is our very important asset, needless to say. I highly recommend Ms. Jeon to your university with great happiness as your program can be beneficial to her further growth.

Yours faithfully,

Vice Dean/Professor of International Trade
Pusan National University

Tommy Lee

November 24, 2022

To the admissions committee,

My name is Dr. Tommy Lee, and I am a professor and dean of the Department of International Trade at the College of Economics and International Trade at Pusan National University. I teach the theory and practice of international trade and logistics. I am delighted to write a letter of recommendation for Sunah Kim, whom I have known for most of her time at PNU. I had the opportunity to observe Sunah demonstrating her outstanding academic and leadership qualities through the Honors Class, mentoring program, and International Internship Program I oversaw. Since Sunah started at our university, she has never wavered in her commitment to learn, giving her best to every assignment and opportunity. She is an extremely intelligent student, and this, combined with her strong work ethic, landed her in the top 1% of students in our school's Honors Class, which recognizes students who excel in both schoolwork and extracurricular activities. Her hard work also paid off in merit scholarships over several semesters and her being given Magna Cum Laude honors upon her graduation. She was the only one of more than 30 students in the International Internship Program to go to New York, and she received an offer for a full-time position and visa sponsorship from VOESH New York.

Her greatest strength is that she sets realistic goals to complete assigned tasks while never taking her eye off of her long-term goals. Soon after I met Sunah, I saw her passion for international trade and realized she needed a steppingstone to a larger world. This prompted me to recommend her for an exchange program in the United States. Following her return from the semester-long internship abroad, she shared with me, with a twinkle in her eye, that she aspired to receive a world-class education and to study and work with people from diverse cultural backgrounds. Later, while preparing for graduation, she received the opportunity for another international internship, and I know that her eventual relocation to New York was the culmination of her extensive preparation and study. I was proud to hear that She overcame cultural differences, learned new things, adapted well, and worked diligently all by herself in an unfamiliar place.

She earned an A+ in three of the four courses I taught, demonstrating her ability to learn quickly and apply her knowledge. She earned excellent grades in International Commercial Transactions, Business English for International Trade, International Transportation, and Customs Law. She demonstrated outstanding ability in applying the complex principles of international trade to the various facets of real-world situations. I was particularly impressed by her paper when she took a course on basic transportation conditions & rules for trade called "Incoterms" in International Commercial Transactions. Her paper clearly described the application of Incoterms to practical situations and analyzed it by referring to various papers and books. During the three years I taught her, she consistently built positive working relationships with her fellow students, even assuming leadership of a departmental group as a freshman. Taking everything into account, I can say that She was one of the best students I've ever taught.

Her transition to Data Science will be yet another beginning. Given Sunah's ambition, enthusiasm for learning, and inquisitive nature, I have no doubt that she will once again excel, adapt, and succeed regardless of school or profession. It was a pleasure to teach her, and I hope my recommendation will aid your decision-making. I am certain that Sunah Kim is one of the best applicants for your program, and I confidently recommend her. Thank you.

Sincerely,

Tommy Lee
Dean of the Department of International Trade
College of Economics and International Trade
Pusan National University

12-5 Concepts and Examples of Job Interview

취업 면접이란

취업 면접은 지원자가 고용되어야 하는지를 평가하기 위해 수행되는 구직자와 고용주 대표 간의 대화로 구성된 면접이다. 면접은 직원 선발의 가장 일반적인 방법 중 하나이다. 면접에 초대되었다는 것은 당신의 지원이 좋은 인상을 주었다는 것을 의미한다. 면접 동안 고용주는 지원자의 자격, 외모 그리고 구직에 대한 일반적인 적합성을 평가할 기회가 있다.

1. What is the Job Interview?

Being invited to an interview means that your application must have made a good impression. A job interview is a conversation which occurs between a potential employer and a job applicant. During the job interview, the employer has the opportunity to appraise applicant's qualifications, appearance and general fitness for the job opening. You need to prepare yourself for the interview to make sure that you are successful.

2. Examples of Job Interview

(1) Tell me about yourself

[Sample 1]

I currently work as a secretary to the general manager in the sales office of a European telecommunications company. Since he doesn't speak Korean, my main function is to act as liaison between him and eight Korean staff members. In addition to general office duties, I also perform accounting, including payrolls. My boss frequently travels and I effectively manage the office during his absence. I'm a self-starter and he fully trusts my ability to work without his supervision and he values my judgment in a variety of contexts.

[Sample 2]

I'm an International Trade major at Pusan National University. After I graduate next February, I'd like to work for an international trading firm. I've traveled to several countries in Asia and Europe. Getting to know other cultures and people is a fascinating experience. I'm currently enrolled in night courses in business English and export-import documentation in order to prepare myself for the field.

(2) What are some of your strengths?

[Sample 1]

My biggest strength is tenacity. All my past employers and business associates have said I am tenacious. I have to see a project through to the finish no matter what challenges I encounter along the way. I always give whatever it takes to complete the job.

[Sample 2]

I'm also highly stress-resistant. I have been working in a stressful environment where I have to meet deadlines constantly. While some people cannot perform well under pressure, I thrive.
The fact that I've always met deadlines and survived stressful situations makes me confident that I can meet any deadline.

[Sample 3]

I have been told I have excellent people skills. I get along well with almost every one and I have no trouble getting to know new people.

[Sample 4]

I have excellent research and analytical skills. I received A's on all the reports I did for marketing classes. For an independent-study project, I researched the air-express industry. The professor said my report was better writing than those written by professional consulting firms. She integrated a large part of my report into her own research report, which was published.

(3) What are some of your weaknesses?

[Sample 1]

I tend to be a perfectionist. While doing the marketing research I just mentioned, I went a bit overboard. I researched over 200 articles and my report was over 100 pages. It was beyond the scope of a four-unit class!

[Sample 2]

I love my work and always give each project 100%, if not 110%. So when I don't feel others are giving their best, I find it a little frustrating.

[Sample 3]

I prefer to see a project through from start to finish, so I sometimes find it a little frustrating to work on a single component and not have something to contribute to all the important aspects of a project.

Key Expressions & Technical Terms

✔ **Resume:** A resume provides a summary of your education, work history, credentials, and other accomplishments and skills. There are also optional sections, including a resume objective and a career summary statement.

✔ **Chronological Resume:** A chronological resume is a standard resume format that lists your work history in reverse chronological order, starting with your most recent job listed at the top and each previous position in descending order.

✔ **Functional Resume:** A functional resume is a type of resume format which showcases skills over experience. The purpose of a functional resume is to draw attention to transferable abilities rather than focusing on a chronological overview of your work history.

✔ **Combination Resume:** A combination resume lists your skills and qualifications first. Your employment history is listed next, in reverse chronological order

✔ **Personal Self Introduction Letter:** A personal self introduction letter is something that you can use to introduce yourself to other people.

✔ **Letter of Rcommendation:** A letter of recommendation is a letter written on behalf of an applicant by someone who can vouch for that person's educational or professional performance.

✔ **Job Interview:** A job interview is a conversation which occurs between a potential employer and a job applicant. During the job interview, the employer has the opportunity to appraise applicant's qualifications, appearance and general fitness for the job opening.

Check-up Questions 12

Q1 Is a resume the same as a CV?

➥

Q2 What do I write in a cover letter?

➥

Q3 What is the format for a letter of recommendation?

➥

Q4 What is the job interview?

➥

Q5 What are some of your strengths and weaknesses?

➥

Index

| 저자약력 |

이양기

부산대학교 상과대학 무역학과 졸업
부산대학교 대학원 무역학과 석사과정 졸업(경제학 석사)
부산대학교 대학원 무역학과 박사과정 졸입(경제학 박사)
한국무역통상학회 회장, 한국무역학회 부회장, 한국무역상무학회 부회장
한국글로벌무역학회 부회장, 한국국제상학회 상임이사, 한국관세학회 상임이사
한국통상정보학회 상임이사, 한국중재학회 상임이사, 한국경제통상학회 이사
한국아시아학회 이사, 한국산업경제학회 이사
전) 관세청 관세사자격시험 출제 및 채점위원
　행정자치부 공무원시험 출제위원
　부산대학교 홍보실장, 입학부본부장, 경제통상대학원 부원장
　한국산업인력공단 물류관리사 자격시험 출제위원
현) 부산대학교 경제통상대학 무역학부장
　부산대학교 경제통상연구원 부원장

〈저서〉

관세법, 박영사 | 무역실무, 삼영사 | 최신무역학원론(공저), 두남
국제상거래론(공저), 박영사 | 무역결제론(공저), 삼영사
알기 쉬운 국제상거래론, 도서출판 청람 | 무역관계법규, 박영사

〈주요 논문〉

- "블록체인 선하증권 운용을 위한 블록체인 플랫폼의 상호 연계 필요성", 『무역상무연구』, 제95권, 한국무역상무학회, 2022.
- "Effect of International Trade and Business for Approval Mediated by Relationship Capabilities on Korea's Export Growth", Journal of Korea Trade, vol.26 no.6, 2022 등 90여 편

[저자 홈페이지] http://trade.pusan.ac.kr

Global Business English

2023년 9월 10일 1판 1쇄 인쇄
2023년 9월 15일 1판 1쇄 발행

저　자 | 이양기
발행인 | 이수성
발행처 | 도서출판 청람
　서울시 마포구 독막로 288(대흥동, 세양상가 109호)
전　화 | 02)3272-2601~2
팩　스 | 02)3272-2603
E-mail | crbooks@daum.net
홈페이지 | http://www.crbooks.co.kr
등　록 | 2000년 8월 26일 제6-0509호

ISBN 978-89-5972-983-8 93320　　[정가 25,000원]